A GUIDE TO
THE MAYOR OF CASTERBRIDGE

MARY HARTLEY
WITH TONY BUZAN

Hodder & Stoughton

Cover photograph ©: BBC Worldwide
Mind Maps: Ann Jones
Illustrations: Karen Donnelly

ISBN 0 340 75325 0

First published 1999
Impression number   10 9 8 7 6 5 4 3 2 1
Year   2002 2001 2000 1999

The 'Teach Yourself' name and logo are registered trade marks of
Hodder & Stoughton Ltd.

Copyright © 1999 Mary Hartley
Introduction ('How to study') copyright © 1998 Tony Buzan

Typeset by Transet Limited, Coventry, England.
Printed in Great Britain for Hodder & Stoughton Educational, a division of
Hodder Headline Plc, 338 Euston Road, London NW1 3BH by Cox and Wyman Ltd,
Reading, Berks.

ONTENTS

There are five important things you must know about your brain and memory to revolutionize the way you study:

◆ how your memory ('recall') works *while* you are learning
◆ how your memory works *after* you have finished learning
◆ how to use Mind Maps – a special technique for helping you with all aspects of your studies
◆ how to increase your reading speed
◆ how to prepare for tests and exams.

Recall during learning
– THE NEED FOR BREAKS

When you are studying, your memory can concentrate, understand and remember well for between 20 and 45 minutes at a time. Then it needs a break. If you carry on for longer than this without a break your memory starts to break down. If you study for hours non-stop, you will remember only a small fraction of what you have been trying to learn, and you will have wasted hours of valuable time.

So, ideally, *study for less than an hour*, then take a five to ten minute break. During the break listen to music, go for a walk, do some exercise, or just daydream. (Daydreaming is a necessary brain-power booster – geniuses do it regularly.) During the break your brain will be sorting out what it has been learning, and you will go back to your books with the new information safely stored and organized in your memory banks. We recommend breaks at regular intervals as you work through the Literature Guides. Make sure you take them!

Recall after learning
– THE WAVES OF YOUR MEMORY

What do you think begins to happen to your memory straight after you have finished learning something? Does it immediately start forgetting? No! Your brain actually *increases* its power and carries on remembering. For a short time after your study session, your brain integrates the information, making a more complete picture of everything it has just learnt. Only then does the rapid decline in memory begin, and as much as 80 per cent of what you have learnt can be forgotten in a day.

However, if you catch the top of the wave of your memory, and briefly review (look back over) what you have been studying at the correct time, the memory is stamped in far more strongly, and stays at the crest of the wave for a much longer time. To maximize your brain's power to remember, take a few minutes and use a Mind Map to review what you have learnt at the end of a day. Then review it at the end of a week, again at the end of a month, and finally a week before your test or exam. That way you'll ride your memory wave all the way there – and beyond!

The Mind Map ®
– A PICTURE OF THE WAY YOU THINK

Do you like taking notes? More important, do you like having to go back over and learn them before tests or exams? Most students I know certainly do not! And how do you take your notes? Most people take notes on lined paper, using blue or black ink. The result, visually, is boring! And what does *your* brain do when it is bored? It turns off, tunes out, and goes to sleep! Add a dash of colour, rhythm, imagination, and the whole note-taking process becomes much more fun, uses more of your brain's abilities, and improves your recall and understanding.

A Mind Map mirrors the way your brain works. It can be used for note-taking from books or in class, for reviewing what you have just studied, and for essay planning for coursework and in tests or exams. It uses all your memory's natural techniques to build up your rapidly growing 'memory muscle'.

You will find Mind Maps throughout this book. Study them, add some colour, personalize them, and then have a go at drawing your own – you'll remember them far better! Stick them in your files and on your walls for a quick-and-easy review of the topic.

HOW TO DRAW A MIND MAP

1 Start in the middle of the page. This gives your brain the maximum room for its thoughts.
2 Always start by drawing a small picture or symbol. Why? Because a picture is worth a thousand words to your brain. And try to use at least three colours, as colour helps your memory even more.
3 Let your thoughts flow, and write or draw your ideas on coloured branching lines connected to your central image. These key symbols and words are the headings for your topic. Start like the Mind Map on page 9.
4 Then add facts and ideas by drawing more, smaller, branches on to the appropriate main branches, just like a tree.
5 Always print your word clearly on its line. Use only one word per line.
6 To link ideas and thoughts on different branches, use arrows, colours, underlining, and boxes (see page 17).

HOW TO READ A MIND MAP

1 Begin in the centre, the focus of your topic.
2 The words/images attached to the centre are like chapter headings; read them next.
3 Always read out from the centre, in every direction (even on the left-hand side, where you will have to read from right to left, instead of the usual left to right).

USING MIND MAPS

Mind Maps are a versatile tool – use them for taking notes in class or from books, for solving problems, for brainstorming with friends, and for reviewing and working for tests or exams – their uses are endless! You will find them invaluable for planning essays for coursework and exams. Number your main branches in the order in which you want to use them and off you go – the main headings for your essay are done and all your ideas are logically organized!

Super speed reading

It seems incredible, but it's been proved – the faster you read, the more you understand and remember! So here are some tips to help you to practise reading faster – you'll cover the ground more quickly, remember more, and have more time left for both work and play.

◆ First read the whole text (whether it's a lengthy book or an exam or test paper) very quickly, to give your brain an overall idea of what's ahead and get it working. (It's like sending out a scout to look at the territory you have to cover – it's much easier when you know what to expect!) Then read the text again for more detailed information.
◆ Have the text a reasonable distance away from your eyes. In this way your eye/brain system will be able to see more at a glance, and will naturally begin to read faster.
◆ Take in groups of words at a time. Rather than reading 'slowly and carefully' read faster, more enthusiastically.
◆ Take in phrases rather than single words while you read.
◆ Use a guide. Your eyes are designed to follow movement, so a thin pencil underneath the lines you are reading, moved smoothly along, will 'pull' your eyes to faster speeds.

Preparing for tests and exams

◆ Review your work systematically. Cram at the start of your course, not the end, and avoid 'exam panic'!
◆ Use Mind Maps throughout your course, and build a Master Mind Map for each subject – a giant Mind Map that summarizes everything you know about the subject.
◆ Use memory techniques such as mnemonics (verses or systems for remembering things like dates and events).
◆ Get together with one or two friends to study, compare Mind Maps, and discuss topics.

AND FINALLY...

Have *fun* while you learn – it has been shown that students who make their studies enjoyable understand and remember everything better and get the highest grades. I wish you and your brain every success! —(Tony Buzan)

This guide assumes that you have already read *The Mayor of Casterbridge*, although you could read 'Background' and 'The story of *The Mayor of Casterbridge*' before that. It is best to use the guide alongside the novel. You could read the 'Who's who?' and 'Themes' sections without referring to the novel, but you will get more out of these sections if you do refer to it too, especially when thinking about the questions designed to test your recall and help you to think about the novel.

The 'Commentary' section can be used in a number of ways. One way is to read a chapter or part of a chapter in the novel, and then read the commentary for that section. Keep on until you come to a test section, test yourself – then have a break! Alternatively, read the Commentary for a chapter, then read that chapter in the novel, then go back to the Commentary.

'Topics for discussion and brainstorming' gives topics that could well feature in exams or provide the basis for coursework. It would be particularly useful for you to discuss them with friends, or brainstorm them using Mind Map techniques (see p. vii).

'How to get an "A" in English Literature' gives valuable advice on what to look for in a text, and what skills you need to develop in order to achieve your personal best.

'The exam essay' is a useful 'night before' reminder of how to tackle exam questions, and 'Model answer' gives an example of an A-grade essay and the Mind Map and plan used to write it.

The questions

Whenever you come across a question in the guide with a star ✪ in front of it, think about it for a moment. You could even jot down a few words in rough to focus your mind. There is not usually a 'right' answer to these questions: it is important for you to develop your own opinions if you want to get an 'A' in your exam. The 'Test yourself' sections are designed to take you about 10–20 minutes each. Take a short break after each one.

KEY TO ICONS

Themes

A **theme** is an idea explored by an author. Whenever a theme is dealt with in the guide, the appropriate icon is used. This means you can find where a theme is mentioned just by flicking through the book. Go on – try it now!

Fate and destiny   Rivalry

Secrecy and deception   Place and setting

Love

STYLE AND LANGUAGE

This heading and icon are used in the Commentary wherever there is a special section on the author's choice of words and imagery.

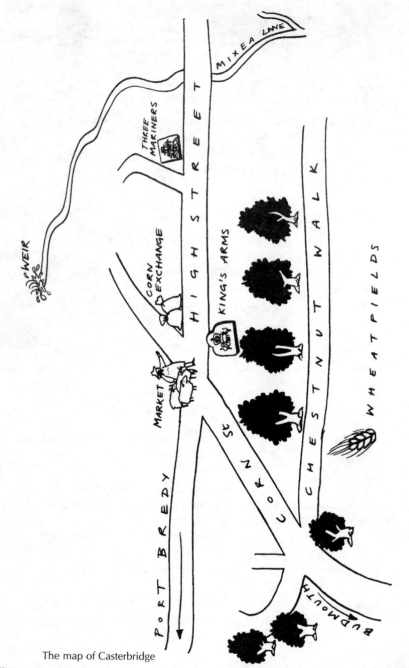

The map of Casterbridge

Thomas Hardy was born in 1840 in Dorset in a small village called Higher Bockhampton. He went to school in the nearby town of Dorchester, which features as Casterbridge in *The Mayor of Casterbridge*. After training as an architect in Dorchester, Hardy worked in an architect's office in London for five years. Although he enjoyed the pleasures of London life and did well in his chosen career, he did not feel at ease in fashionable city society and returned to Dorset in 1867. Some of the sad experiences in his life are reflected in the gloomy tone of much of his work, including *The Mayor of Casterbridge*. He lost his religious faith and came to see human beings as powerless victims of chance and fate; he was uncomfortably aware of his humble background; a close friend committed suicide; his first marriage was unhappy. However, Hardy's depiction of country life and people is full of warmth and humanity, and some of the scenes in *The Mayor of Casterbridge* celebrate his country heritage.

Changing times

Hardy lived through a period of great social upheaval and technical change. England was changing from being an agricultural country and becoming increasingly industrialized. In *The Mayor of Casterbridge* Farfrae introduces new machinery to the town (see Chapter 24), and his business-like approach to managing a corn dealership reflects the new style of trading.

Corn Laws

Although the novel was published in 1886, it is set around 1820. In the period of the story farmers were protected by the Corn Laws, which imposed duties on imported foreign corn. Many farmers enjoyed wealth and prosperity. The Corn Laws were repealed in 1846, making farming more competitive. The old way of trading, as demonstrated by Henchard's practices, of dealing by word of mouth and measuring in handspans and rough guesses became increasingly obsolete. More business-like methods of the kind illustrated by Farfrae became necessary for prosperity in the changing world of agriculture.

Rural life

THE MARKET-PLACE

Casterbridge is a busy country town with a thriving market-place and a range of inhabitants of different types and classes. The descriptions of items in the shop windows (see Chapter 4) show *the agricultural and pastoral character* of the town. The mornings of market-days are dominated by the farmers and moneyed classes who travel in gigs and vans to trade their goods and livestock for large amounts of money. The most important have official stalls with their names displayed: Henchard, Shiner, Everdene (read *Far From the Madding Crowd* to find out who this is!) to which the name Farfrae is added (see Chapter 17). Later in the day, the poor people who travel on foot with just a few pence to spend are seen. The market-place is the hub of activity, where farmers, merchants, dairymen and hawkers gather to barter and trade. In Chapter 22 we see gathered at Casterbridge market a wine merchant, a horse dealer, a pig-breeder, an auctioneer and millers, all watched by Lucetta and Elizabeth-Jane through the window.

Customs and traditions

FAIRS

Fairs like the one at Weydon Priors where Henchard sold Susan were annual events, although wife-selling was not the norm! Cattle and horses would be sold at the fairs which attracted a variety of travellers and traders. The description of the Weydon Priors Fair refers to the *peep-shows, toy-stands, waxworks and inspired monsters* which provided entertainment for the crowds and money for the stallholders. (See Chapter 1)

SKIMMINGTON-RIDES

A skimmington- or skimmity-ride was a noisy procession intended to ridicule a woman or her husband in situations where one was unfaithful to or ill-treated the other. Apparently the name came from the ladle used to skim milk, which the woman would use to hit the man. Hardy's account of this rural custom shows effigies dressed like the people involved (Lucetta and Henchard) propped up on a donkey. The donkey is led through the town to the accompaniment of tambourines, rams'-horns, fiddles and other ancient musical instruments (see Chapter 39).

Superstitions

Henchard is not the only superstitious character in the novel. Five other farmers consult the weather-prophet about the harvest (see Chapter 26). Many people pretend to dismiss the predictions but secretly believe in them. Mr Fall the weather-prophet is a kind of witch who not only predicts future events but offers cures for warts and similar ailments. The *toad-bag* refers to the belief that toads' legs worn in a bag around the neck would cure disease.

Church and social values

In Casterbridge, religion is a part of life. Henchard swears his oath in a church and keeps his vow religiously. Hardy refers to *the steady churchgoers of the town* (see Chapter 33) whose conversation in the Three Mariners on Sundays focuses on the quality of the morning's sermon. There are firmly held ideas about sexual and social behaviour, particularly where women are concerned. Lucetta's reputation would be ruined if her past relationship with Henchard emerged.

Publication

Hardy's novels were usually printed in serial form in magazines before being published as books. His readers expected a weekly instalment full of events with a dramatic ending to each part. Hardy himself thought that *The Mayor of Casterbridge* was spoilt by too many incidents. ✪ Do you agree with him?

THE STORY OF *THE MAYOR OF CASTERBRIDGE*

Michael Henchard, a poor young **hay-trusser**, gets drunk at a fair and sells his wife **Susan** and his baby daughter **Elizabeth-Jane** to a **sailor**, **Richard Newson**. The trio leave and emigrate to **Canada**. After searching for them in vain, Henchard vows to **abstain from alcohol** for **twenty-one** years.

TOGETHER AGAIN

About **eighteen** years later Susan and her daughter return. Susan thinks that Newson has **drowned**, and wants to find Henchard and ask him to help them. Susan is directed to **Casterbridge**, where Henchard is now the **Mayor** and a thriving **corn-dealer**. Susan and Henchard meet secretly and Henchard offers to establish Susan in a cottage and to **court and marry** her publicly. In this way he will right the wrong that was done all those years ago. **Elizabeth-Jane** does not know anything of their previous history, and thinks of the dead **Newson** as her **father**.

THE RIVAL

Donald Farfrae arrives in town, passing through, and gives **Henchard** advice about a problem he is having with his **corn**. Henchard persuades Farfrae to stay on as his **corn manager**. The two men become **friends**, Henchard in particular being very **fond** of the young man. Henchard confides to **Farfrae** the story of Susan and of his past relationship with **Lucetta**, a woman he had known in **Jersey**. Henchard, believing Susan to be dead, had promised to marry **Lucetta**. **Farfrae** helps Henchard to write an explanation of the new situation to send to **Lucetta**. **Henchard** marries **Susan**.

NOT MY DAUGHTER

Susan dies. Henchard tells Elizabeth-Jane that she is his **daughter**, but then finds a letter from **Susan** telling him that Elizabeth-Jane is, in fact, **Newson's** daughter. **Henchard's** own daughter had died shortly after the auction. Bitterly disappointed, he **rejects** Elizabeth-Jane, who has no idea why he is behaving so coldly towards her. Rivalry develops between him and **Farfrae**, and the younger man sets up a business in competition with **Henchard**.

ENTER LUCETTA

Lucetta comes to Casterbridge, hoping to **marry** Henchard. She also wants him to return the **letters** she had written to him. **Farfrae** and Lucetta fall in love. When Henchard realizes this, he bullies Lucetta into **promising to marry** him. His past is revealed by the **furmity woman** who had witnessed the auction of Susan, and **Lucetta** hastily marries **Farfrae**.

FARFRAE THE WINNER

Henchard's business fails and he becomes **bankrupt**. **Farfrae** buys his **business**, his **house** and his **furniture**, and employs Henchard as a **hay-trusser**. Henchard takes lodgings with **Jopp**, his former manager. **Farfrae** becomes **Mayor**. The period of Henchard's vow comes to an end and he starts to **drink**.

SKIMMINGTON-RIDE

Lucetta asks again for her **letters**. Henchard gives them to **Jopp** to deliver, but Jopp **reads the letters** to the locals in a pub. The locals decide to shame **Lucetta** and **Henchard** by staging a **skimmington-ride**. **Farfrae** is sent a note to get him out of the way, but **Lucetta** sees the ride and **collapses in a fit**. Farfrae returns just before **Lucetta dies**.

THE FINAL DEFEAT

Henchard softens towards **Elizabeth-Jane** and they become close – but then **Newson** returns. Henchard tells him that Elizabeth-Jane is **dead**, and Newson **goes away**. Henchard is depressed and suicidal. **Newson** reappears and **Henchard** leaves Casterbridge. **Farfrae** marries Elizabeth-Jane. **Henchard** returns for the **wedding**, but Elizabeth-Jane, angry and distressed by his deceptions, sends him away. Elizabeth-Jane **regrets** her treatment of Henchard and searches for him, but arrives **too late**. Henchard has died, a sad and broken man.

THE STORY OF THE MAYOR OF CASTERBRIDGE

connections between events

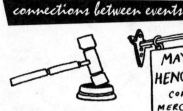

1 Henchard sells Susan and daughter and they leave with Newson

2 18 years later, Susan and daughter arrive

3 Susan and Henchard marry

4 Farfrae, Henchard's manager, sets up his own business and rivalry develops

5 Susan dies; Henchard finds out that Elizabeth is not his daughter.

6 Henchard's old flame Lucetta returns — but falls for Farfrae; soon they marry.

7 Farfrae succeeds and Henchard becomes bankrupt. Farfrae takes Henchard's place.

8 Lucetta's old affair is exposed and she dies

9 Newson returns to find Elizabeth-Jane

10 Henchard leaves, depressed and defeated

11 Henchard returns for the wedding but Elizabeth-Jane rejects him and he leaves

12 Elizabeth-Jane changes her mind but too late. Henchard dies alone and bitter.

How much can you remember?

Try to fill in the words missing in this summary without looking at the original. Use your own words if they have the same meaning.

_____ _____, a poor young _____, gets drunk at a fair and sells his wife _____ and his baby daughter _____ to a _____ _____ _____. The trio leave and emigrate to _____. After searching for them in vain, Henchard vows to _____ _____ _____ for _____ years.

TOGETHER AGAIN

About _____ years later Susan and her daughter return. Susan thinks that Newson has _____, and wants to find Henchard and ask him to help them. Susan is directed to _____, where Henchard is now the _____ and a thriving _____. Susan and Henchard meet secretly and Henchard offers to establish Susan in a cottage and to _____ _____ _____ her publicly. In this way he will right the wrong that was done all those years ago. _____ does not know anything of their previous history, and thinks of the dead _____ as her _____.

THE RIVAL

_____ _____ arrives in town, passing through, and gives _____ advice about a problem he is having with his _____. Henchard persuades Farfrae to stay on as his _____ _____. The two men become _____ , Henchard in particular being very _____ of the young man. Henchard confides to _____ the story of Susan and of his past relationship with _____, a woman he had known in _____. Henchard, believing Susan to be dead, had promised to marry _____. _____ helps Henchard to write an explanation of the new situation to send to _____ . _____ marries _____.

NOT MY DAUGHTER

_____ dies. Henchard tells Elizabeth-Jane that she is his _____, but then finds a letter from _____ telling him that Elizabeth-Jane is, in fact, _____ daughter. _____ own daughter had died shortly after the auction. Bitterly disappointed, he _____ Elizabeth-Jane, who has no idea why he is behaving so coldly towards her. Rivalry develops between him

7

and _____, and the younger man sets up a business in competition with _____.

ENTER LUCETTA

Lucetta comes to Casterbridge, hoping to _____ Henchard. She also wants him to return the _____ she had written to him. _____ and Lucetta fall in love. When Henchard realizes this he bullies Lucetta into _____ _____ _____ him. His past is revealed by the _____ _____ who had witnessed the auction of Susan, and _____ hastily marries _____.

FARFRAE THE WINNER

Henchard's business fails and he becomes _____. _____ buys his _____, his _____ and his _____, and employs Henchard as a _____ . Henchard takes lodgings with _____, his former manager. _____ becomes _____. The period of Henchard's vow comes to an end and he starts to _____.

SKIMMINGTON-RIDE

Lucetta asks again for her _____. Henchard gives them to _____ to deliver, but Jopp _____ _____ _____ to the locals in a pub. The locals decide to shame _____ and _____ by staging a _____. _____ is sent a note to get him out of the way, but _____ sees the ride and _____. Farfrae returns just before _____ _____.

THE FINAL DEFEAT

Henchard softens towards _____ and they become close – but then _____ returns. Henchard tells him that Elizabeth-Jane is _____, and Newson _____ _____ . Henchard is depressed and suicidal. _____ reappears and _____ leaves Casterbridge. _____ marries Elizabeth-Jane. _____ returns for the _____, but Elizabeth-Jane, angry and distressed by his deception, sends him away. Elizabeth-Jane _____ her treatment of Henchard and searches for him, but arrives _____ _____. Henchard has died, a sad and broken man.

Now you're clear about the story, take a break before exploring the characters.

The Mini Mind Map above summarizes the characters in *The Mayor of Casterbridge*. Test yourself by looking at the full Mind Map on p. 17, and then copying the Mini Mind Map and trying to add to it from memory.

Michael Henchard

AN EMOTIONAL MAN

The name 'Henchard' fits the character: it sounds like 'Wrench hard'. Henchard's personality dominates the novel. His character is larger than life, exhibiting extreme swings of mood and emotion. He behaves impulsively, not stopping to think of the consequences of his actions. Examples of Henchard's impulsive behaviour are the sale of his wife, his treatment of Abel Whittle and his dismissal of Jopp. Henchard is ruled by feeling rather than thought, and is often the victim of his own passions. We are told that he *knew no moderation in his requests and impulses* (Chapter 12). Henchard loves Elizabeth-Jane when he thinks she is his child, and violently turns against her when he discovers her real parentage, never stopping to consider that this circumstance is hardly her fault! Similarly, his great affection for Farfrae turns into great hatred which Farfrae hardly deserves. Henchard cannot control his jealous and envious outbursts, which eventually alienate his former friend.

AN HONOURABLE MAN

Although Henchard can behave cruelly, as when he sells his wife and turns against Elizabeth-Jane, he can also act in a kind and honourable way. He does show a sense of responsibility towards Susan, Elizabeth-Jane and Lucetta, and tries to make up for the wrongs he has done them. Henchard's plan of setting up a household for Susan and then openly courting her (Chapter 11) shows concern for her reputation. Henchard has the power to harm his hated rival, Farfrae, when he reads out Lucetta's letters and when he gets the upper hand of Farfrae in the fight in the granary, but he cannot bring himself to push home his advantage. Henchard could also destroy the romance between Farfrae and Elizabeth-Jane by revealing that she is legally nobody's child. Henchard's moral sense guides him in these instances. Also, Henchard keeps Abel Whittle's mother supplied with good quality coal and with snuff (Chapter 15), and he sells his last remaining possession, his watch, to pay one of his poor creditors.

A MAN TO BE PITIED

Henchard has many faults. He is more or less incapable of moderating his responses, and says what he feels without applying judgement. At the same time, he cannot express his deepest feelings in words, relying instead on actions which can be rough and brutal: *Loving a man or hating him, his diplomacy was as wrong-headed as a buffalo's*. Nevertheless, Henchard gains our sympathy. He makes mistakes but experiences great suffering as a result. He is unable to ward off the disastrous results of his passions and prejudices, and has to learn to accept the workings of fate. In Chapter 19 we read that he is constantly aware of *some sinister intelligence bent on punishing him*. Henchard's need to show love is frustrated throughout the novel, and he dies an isolated, lonely figure.

Donald Farfrae

Hardy probably chose the name 'Farfrae' because in Scots dialect it means 'far from': Farfrae is far from home. Farfrae presents a contrast to Henchard, both in temperament and in the pattern of his fortunes, moving upwards in life as

Henchard moves down. On his arrival in Casterbridge, Farfrae is immediately popular, enthralling the locals at the Three Mariners with his singing and attracting the attention of Elizabeth-Jane. Farfrae's association with song and dance throughout the novel suggests a warm and outgoing nature, although in fact he is moderate and reserved. His delight in songs and dances may show shallow sentimentality rather than deep feeling.

GOOD AT BUSINESS

Farfrae is a good businessman, educated and forward-thinking. He understands the new technology, and brings order to Henchard's business affairs. He is also fair in his dealings with other people, as illustrated by his intervention when Henchard is humiliating Abel Whittle. Possibly the calculating nature which stands Farfrae in good stead in business does not appear so attractive when seen in his personal life. The fact that Farfrae pays less than Henchard does not matter to the workers because Farfrae is an easier and more consistent master (Chapter 31), but his reluctance to *make a hole in a sovereign* when searching for Henchard in Chapter 45 is unappealing.

FRIENDLY RIVAL

Farfrae is generous and fair in his dealings with Henchard. Even after the fight he tries to help Henchard by setting him up in the seedshop, and he offers Henchard accommodation in his house. In contrast to Henchard, Farfrae bears no resentment – perhaps because he does not become so emotionally involved with people. He does fall for Lucetta, it is true, but the *insight, briskness and rapidity of his nature* enables him to get over his loss, and he can resume his relationship with Elizabeth-Jane. Farfrae's lack of deep feelings means that his life is free from the emotional turmoil that characterizes Henchard's life, but it also means that we do not view him with the same compassion.

Susan Henchard (Newson)

Susan appears to be a passive, weak woman, rather simple-minded. Henchard has contempt for her because of her simplicity, and even Newson says that she *was not what they call shrewd or sharp at all,* and calls her simple-minded (Chapter 41). We see her lack of sophistication in her belief that Newson had acquired a moral and legal right to her through his purchase. However, it only takes a friend's ridicule to shatter this belief, and Susan's *meek conscience* is troubled until she hears that Newson is lost at sea. Susan appears to be easily influenced and to have no influence over events that happen to her. She is nicknamed *The Ghost* by the boys of Casterbridge because of her pale appearance, and she is generally thought to be weak and fragile.

SURPRISINGLY STRONG

On the other hand, Susan displays surprising strength and spirit. She does try to stop Henchard going ahead with the auction and gives him a firm ultimatum before she leaves with Newson. Susan flings her wedding ring in Henchard's face, saying she is sick of his temper and will try her luck elsewhere. The close glance that Susan gives Newson suggests that she is assessing his character and deciding that he will treat her better than her ill-tempered, discontented husband has done – and indeed, Newson turns out to be a good husband and father.

ALL FOR HER DAUGHTER

Susan, driven by a *desperate effort to advance Elizabeth* (Chapter 4) shows determination and shrewdness in her actions to secure a good future for her daughter. She ascertains *how he stands in the town* before approaching Henchard and maintains the deception about Elizabeth-Jane's age and parentage, even when Henchard asks about the girl's colouring in Chapter 14. Susan also influences Elizabeth-Jane into keeping the name of Newson. Susan takes further steps to secure a settled future for her daughter when she engineers a meeting between Elizabeth-Jane and Farfrae (Chapter 17, 18).

GETS WHAT SHE WANTS

Susan herself is in poor health and *growing thoroughly weary* of life when she comes to Casterbridge, and directs her energy to improving Elizabeth-Jane's prospects. Although she may seem to be an ineffectual shadowy figure, Susan gets what she wants for her daughter, and at her death has achieved the socially respectable position of being the Mayor's wife.

Elizabeth-Jane

Elizabeth-Jane shows strength of character throughout the novel. In her early life she learns to endure poverty and to accept hardship without complaining. Elizabeth-Jane is a serious young woman, *characterized by earnestness and soberness of mien*. She is steady and consistent, and does not allow herself to be carried away by her fortunate position in Henchard's household. We can admire Elizabeth-Jane's attempts to improve herself through study, and her willingness to lend a hand, as when she waits on tables at the inn or does menial tasks at home. Having experienced poverty and oppression, Elizabeth-Jane is careful not to tempt Providence by being self-indulgent or having great expectations of life.

A SHREWD OBSERVER

Elizabeth-Jane is guided by her *innate perceptiveness*. Her thoughtful, reflective nature makes her a reliable observer of events and people. On occasion we view scenes through Elizabeth-Jane's eyes and accept her interpretation of them. Her *seer's spirit* enables her to see the relationship between Farfrae and Lucetta, piecing observations together *like a discerning silent witch* (Chapter 24). Elizabeth-Jane realizes that Henchard should not employ Jopp, and in Chapter 34 she warns Farfrae of Henchard's hostility towards him.

A LOVING 'DAUGHTER'

Elizabeth-Jane is concerned for Henchard's welfare and shows him affection and regard even when hurt and baffled by his behaviour towards her. She stands by him when misfortune strikes and looks after him when he is sick. However, she rejects Henchard when he is most in need of love and forgiveness (Chapter 44). Her words to him are harsh and also exaggerated – Newson was not heartbroken by the false story of her death. Elizabeth-Jane's strict sense of morality and propriety in this instance lead to rigid judgement and lack of compassion.

HAPPY AT LAST?

Elizabeth-Jane patiently accepts the marriage of Lucetta and Farfrae, and is eventually rewarded by marrying Farfrae herself. Marriage brings her *equable serenity*, but she is always aware that happiness is fleeting and temporary.

Lucetta (La Sueur) Templeman

Lucetta is a colourful figure who provides a strong contrast with Susan and Elizabeth-Jane. She met Henchard in Jersey and cared for him through a period of depression. The intimate relationship that developed when they fell in love brought scandal on Lucetta. Lucetta is *of good family, well bred and well educated* (Chapter 12) but these qualities are not emphasized in her portrayal in the novel. Lucetta's *practised manner* and her taste for fashionable clothes and furniture highlight her sophistication and her shallowness. Lucetta is a *dark-haired, large-eyed pretty woman* who is very aware of the impression she makes on others and uses people to her own advantage. For example, Lucetta invites Elizabeth-Jane to live with her in order to attract Henchard to the house, but then has the *disagreeable necessity* of getting rid of her. She abandons Henchard when she falls for Farfrae and marries him in secret while still promised to Henchard, giving as her excuse: *'I knew I should lose Donald if I did not secure him at once'*.

Lucetta is motivated by her passionate nature and her desire to avoid the scandal of her past intimacy with Henchard. In spite of her anxiety, Lucetta seems unable to conquer her addiction to letter writing and continually risks discovery. She sends notes to Henchard and arranges secret meetings. However, it is the original letters to Henchard that prove to be her downfall. Fallen into Jopp's hands, they provoke the skimmington-ride, the effect of which leads to Lucetta's death.

Richard Newson

Newson's first appearance at the furmity tent establishes him as kind and good tempered. His good nature is seen in his friendliness to the Peter's Finger regulars and to Henchard when he arrives at Casterbridge searching for news of his family. Newson shows thoughtfulness and sensitivity in his decision to stay out of Susan's life when he knows her conscience is troubled by their relationship. His kind and trusting nature means that he believes what Henchard tells him. Even when he discovers the lie, he blames himself for being such a *simpleton* as to fall for the story, and calls Henchard a *poor fellow* (Chapter 43). He forgives Henchard, and dismisses his lie as a *good joke*. The genial and warm-hearted sailor moves away from Casterbridge because he wants to live near the sea.

Joshua Jopp

Jopp plays a minor but significant role in the novel. He always seems to be associated with trouble, although he is not always to blame. We first see him when he arrives to keep an appointment with Henchard only to be told that the manager's job has been given to someone else. Jopp is angry and disappointed, and has reason to feel bitter towards both Henchard and Farfrae. Henchard later hires Jopp to be his foreman to cut Farfrae out of business, but when Henchard's plan doesn't work, Jopp gets the blame and is sacked. He vows that Henchard will be sorry for this. He is a frustrated figure, unsuccessful in life, living in the disreputable Mixen Lane. In spite of the ill-feeling between the two men Henchard goes to live with Jopp when he loses his own house.

When Jopp asks Lucetta to recommend him to Farfrae for work, Lucetta brushes him aside. This goads Jopp into seeking revenge. Having been in Jersey at the same time as them, he knows a little of Lucetta's and Henchard's background, and uses the letters entrusted to him to expose the pair. However, the tragic result of the skimmington-ride leaves Jopp ridden with anxiety.

Abel Whittle

Abel works for Henchard. He is a *round shouldered blinking young man of nineteen or twenty* who finds it hard to get up in the mornings. When Henchard treats him harshly for failing to turn up on time Farfrae intervenes on Abel's behalf (Chapter

15). This causes a clash between Henchard and Farfrae. In Chapter 31 we learn through Abel that Farfrae, who has taken over Henchard's business, is a better employer than Henchard. He pays less, but the workers have a more peaceful existence. Abel takes care of Henchard at the end of his life, wishing to repay Henchard for his kindness to Abel's mother.

The rustics

This group of local inhabitants and workers, which includes Abel Whittle, Christopher Coney, Buzzford, Mother Cuxsom and Nance Mockridge, form a chorus (in Greek drama the chorus was a group of people who commented on the action and major characters). The rustics make outspoken and perceptive comments, often humorous, on the action and characters. For example, their remarks at Henchard's marriage to Susan add humour and remind us how ill-matched the pair seems. In Chapter 8, Christopher Coney's response to Farfrae's singing in the Three Mariners: *'What did ye come away from yer own country for, young maister, if ye be so wownded about it?'* alerts us to Farfrae's sentimentality: he is fond of his country, but not enough to go back there.

This group offers poignant words at dramatic moments. Mother Cuxsom's summing-up of Susan's death: *'Well, poor soul; she's helpless to hinder that or anything now'* is both tender and matter of fact, and contrasts with Coney's justification of taking the pennies: *'Why should death rob life o' fourpence?'* Abel Whittle's account of Henchard's last days and hours contains reminders of loyalty, forgiveness and kindness that emphasize the tragedy.

The rustics also make an important contribution to the plot. Abel Whittle's lateness at work is the cause of Henchard and Farfrae clashing. The skimmington-ride is planned by some of the least respectable of the group, and Farfrae is kept away from it by the intervention of others who think it is *too rough a joke*.

17

Pull it together

? Draw a pie chart that includes the major characters. Divide the pie to reflect the amount of sympathy you feel for each character.

? Test yourself using the Mini Mind Map on p. 9 and the full Mind Map on the previous page, as suggested at the start of the chapter.

Now that you've brushed up on the characters, take a break before looking at the themes.

THEMES

A **theme** is an idea developed or explored throughout a work. The Mini Mind Map above shows the main themes of *The Mayor of Casterbridge*. Test yourself by copying the Mini Mind Map, adding to it, and then comparing your results with the version on p. 27.

Fate and destiny

Hardy became unsure of the existence of God and placed his belief in the workings of fate, or destiny. Other words to describe this idea are chance, or providence. Hardy's characters are affected by events which shape their lives in particular ways, over which they have no control. Indeed, the workings of fate seem to mock and frustrate people's own ambitions and efforts.

The plot of *The Mayor of Casterbridge* hinges on a number of coincidences. Some of these have to do with timing. Newson arrives at the furmity tent just as the auction of Susan is taking place. ✪ What would have happened if Newson had not turned up at that precise moment? What might have happened if his ship had not set sail for Canada the very next day? Another fateful arrival is Farfrae's first appearance in Casterbridge. Farfrae happens to arrive just as Henchard is being criticized for the quality of the bread. Farfrae's generous, impulsive gesture in writing Henchard the note offering help sets the subsequent events in motion. ✪ What if Farfrae had not heard the conversation? What is he doing in Casterbridge? Where is he going? Fate causes Henchard's effigy to rise to the top of the water just as he is about to kill himself, giving him a sign that he should not take his life (Chapter 41). Another well-timed coincidence is Henchard's arrival in Chapter 29 just in time to save Elizabeth-Jane and Lucetta from the bull. By an **ironic** twist of fate, Henchard unknowingly has saved Farfrae's wife.

We see the cruel timing of fate on several occasions. On the very same day that Henchard tells Elizabeth-Jane he is her father, he finds the letter telling him that he is not. Henchard asks Elizabeth-Jane to live with him just 10 minutes after she has decided to move in with Lucetta. In Chapter 40, just as Henchard is softening towards Elizabeth-Jane and she appears as a *pin-point of light* in his gloom, Newson turns up. Perhaps the cruellest of all fateful timings is at the end when Elizabeth-Jane finds Henchard just half an hour too late, and he dies without knowing that she loves and forgives him.

The weather seems to conspire against Henchard. The national holiday turns out to be a wet day (Chapter 16). This circumstance means that Henchard's entertainment is a failure and Farfrae's is a success. Even more crucial are the changes in the weather in Chapters 26 and 27 when the rain forecast by the weather-prophet finally arrives, but too late to stop Henchard losing all his money.

Henchard himself believes that he is a victim of fate. He does endure a series of successive blows which suggests that he has been singled out for cruel treatment. In Chapter 27 Henchard ponders: *'I wonder if it can be that somebody has been roasting a waxen image of me, or stirring an unholy brew to confound me.'* ✪ Is the rise and fall of Henchard caused by fate? Does his own character contribute to his destiny?

Secrecy and deception

Many characters in the novel have secrets, some of which they are desperate to keep. The sale of Susan and Elizabeth-Jane is kept secret for 20 years until the chance event of the furmity woman's appearance in court that leads to the secret being revealed. A significant effect of the revelation is that it makes Lucetta decide that she cannot keep her promise to marry Henchard, and that she must marry Farfrae immediately. It also marks the turn in Henchard's fortunes. Following the disclosure of his past, *he passed the ridge of prosperity and honour, and began to descend rapidly on the other side* (Chapter 31). Hardy makes the interesting observation that if the story had been known from the beginning it would now be *lightly regarded* as the one wild oat sown by a respectable mature citizen in his far-off youth.

Deceptions about parentage affect the plot. Susan does not let Henchard know that his own daughter died three months after the auction and that Elizabeth-Jane is the child of Susan and Newson. Susan's letter (Chapter 19) reveals the secret and explains that she had acted for the best, but the effect on Henchard is devastating. He compounds the deception by not telling Elizabeth-Jane the truth. After a series of emotional struggles Henchard decides he can love Elizabeth-Jane anyway, but at this very point Newson returns and Henchard knows that the secret will be revealed. Henchard's desperate lie that Elizabeth-Jane is dead contributes to his final downfall, being part of the reason for Elizabeth-Jane's rejection of him.

Lucetta's desire to keep her past a secret becomes particularly acute when she wants to marry Farfrae. She thinks she is safe when she burns her letters, little knowing that they have already been made public and that her past will be exposed in the skimmity-ride. Lucetta's life in Casterbridge is shrouded in deception and secrecy. She changes her name from Lucette La Sueur to Lucetta Templeman, and tries to present herself to

Casterbridge as a lady from Bath, hiding her previous connection with Jersey. It is amusing to see Lucetta making a great effort not to give herself away by slipping into the French language (Chapter 22), but the strain and anxiety of maintaining her deceptions contributes to her death.

Love

The Mayor of Casterbridge is full of passionate feelings, but on the whole they are not inspired by romantic love. The first picture of Henchard and Susan, walking in silence on the road to Weydon Priors, draws attention to the lacklustre nature of their marriage. Susan's declaration that in the two years she has lived with Henchard she has had *nothing but temper* confirms our impression that theirs is not a happy marriage. When the couple 'remarry' it is not for love. Susan wants to advance Elizabeth-Jane's prospects in life, and Henchard wants to make up for his previous unkindness. He is motivated not by love of Susan but by his desire to do the right thing. Henchard is known for his *haughty indifference to the society of womankind*, and arranges the marriage to Susan in a *dogged unflinching spirit*. In the same way, Henchard is willing to marry Lucetta out of a sense of obligation. Henchard does feel a kind of brotherly love for Farfrae and paternal love for Elizabeth-Jane, and he is more emotionally involved with these two characters than with either of the women in his life.

Lucetta seems to have felt passionately for Henchard. She tells Henchard that she had a *foolish girl's passion* for him. One of her many letters says that she is *unconventionally devoted* to him and feels it impossible that she can marry anyone else. Lucetta is genuinely attracted to Farfrae. When she meets him she is longing for a peaceful, secure relationship: *Her heart longed for some ark into which it could fly and be at rest*.

Farfrae marries two women in the course of the novel, but how strongly does he feel for either of them? His first choice is Elizabeth-Jane. In Chapter 17, Farfrae seems to be about to begin courtship of Elizabeth-Jane, but his interest in her is cut short by Henchard's command that Farfrae should discontinue his attentions. When Henchard withdraws his objections, Farfrae decides to propose to Elizabeth-Jane. His feelings are hardly passionate: he thinks that Elizabeth-Jane is *pleasing, thrifty and satisfactory,* and that marriage to her will reconcile him with Henchard. However, Farfrae becomes infatuated with Lucetta and forgets about Elizabeth-Jane until after Lucetta's death. The ease with which Farfrae transfers his affections from one woman to the other then back again suggests shallow romanticism and practicality rather than deep feelings.

Elizabeth-Jane is interested in Farfrae from their first encounter in the Three Mariners. She watches him from her room in Henchard's house overlooking the hay-stores and granaries. In Chapter 17 we see Elizabeth-Jane's excited and girlish response to Farfrae's words after the dance. She plays games with a scrap of his writing, laughs at herself for being silly, and dresses up in the clothes she had worn to see if her appearance would have attracted Farfrae. However, Elizabeth-Jane convinces herself that the most Farfrae can feel for her is *fleeting regard,* and tries to stop thinking about him. Her eventual marriage to Farfrae is described as putting her in a *latitude of calm weather.* Love brings Elizabeth-Jane a muted kind of happiness.

Rivalry

The rivalry between Henchard and Farfrae is the backbone of the novel. Henchard is immediately drawn to Farfrae, both as a prospective corn manager and as a person. Henchard is lonely (see Chapter 8 and Chapter 12) and his *sudden liking* for Farfrae shows his need for friendship. At first, the difference in the two men's characters doesn't matter. Henchard is captivated by Farfrae's *curious mixture of romance and thrift* (Chapter 38). Henchard's warmth and *tigerish affection* sometimes cause him to become too domineering, but he checks himself when he realizes that he has gone too far (see Chapter 14). Henchard admires Farfrae's cleverness and benefits from the improved business systems that Farfrae introduces. Henchard walks with his arm across Farfrae's shoulder *as if Farfrae were a younger brother.*

The two men clash over Henchard's treatment of Abel Whittle and a strain enters their relationship. When Farfrae's entertainment is a great success and Henchard's is a wash-out, Henchard, full of jealousy, suggests that Farfrae should leave his employment. Farfrae opens his own business, which grows from strength to strength. Farfrae's success and popularity increase as Henchard's decline. When Henchard becomes bankrupt Farfrae buys his business, his house and his possessions. However, Farfrae maintains friendly relations with Henchard; *he had never so passionately liked Henchard as Henchard had liked him* (Chapter 35) and so can be friendly without being emotional. Henchard is tormented by resentment and jealousy, made worse by his affectionate feelings for Farfrae. In Chapter 38 Henchard's bitterness culminates in the fight with Farfrae, which he immediately regrets, tormented by the thought that Farfrae once thought highly of him and now will hate and despise him.

Henchard also sees Farfrae as a rival in his personal life. Lucetta does promise to marry him, but when Henchard asks her to help him to buy time from a creditor by announcing their immediate marriage, she has to reveal that she has already married Farfrae. Henchard fears that Farfrae will take Elizabeth-Jane away from him, too blinded by envy and resentment to see the advantages of a union between his step-daughter and his old friend and competitor.

We may see Lucetta and Elizabeth-Jane as rivals for Farfrae, although Lucetta is unaware of the other's interest. Elizabeth-Jane accepts Farfrae's interest in Lucetta, thinking it quite natural that he should find Lucetta more attractive than her.

Place and setting

Casterbridge itself is an important part of the novel. The descriptions of the shops and the market-place make us aware that Casterbridge is an agricultural town. Even at the dinner parties of the professional families, we are told, the subjects of discussion were *corn, cattle disease, sowing and reaping, fencing and planting*. The town and its people are brought alive through the references to local customs, the use of dialect and the detail with which the local architecture and the urban and rural landscapes are presented. In many scenes the **setting** is an important part of the action, reflecting the moods and behaviour of the characters in the novel.

Casterbridge is an ancient Roman town, seeming to be *shut in by a square wall of trees* (Chapter 4), limes and chestnuts. Picture it in your mind's eye (a useful technique for other scenes, too). The town has no suburbs, but is surrounded by miles *of rotund down and concave field*, and seems to complement the rural life around it. Bees and butterflies abound in the High Street in summer, and in the autumn, leaves and thistledown are blown along it. Town life and country life merge together in Casterbridge. We are told in Chapter 14 that a farmer's boy in the fields can throw a stone into the office window of the town clerk, and that reapers working among the sheaves of corn can greet their friends standing on the corner of the pavement.

The Ring, or ampitheatre, is the town's dominant characteristic. This historic circle is accessible from every part of the town and is the scene of many a secret meeting. The Ring is described as *melancholy, impressive, lonely*, and it is associated with violence and tragedy. For many years it had been the site of the town gallows, and more recently *fights almost to the death* have taken place in the arena. We are told that happy lovers never meet here. The Ring provides the gloomy background for Henchard's meetings with Susan in Chapter 11 and Lucetta in Chapter 35.

Another dismal area of the town is formed by its north-east precincts. Unlike the cheerful avenues in the south of the town, this area is *sunless, even in summer time.* Here the river runs beneath a low cliff, through a meadow bordering what used to be the county gaol. The cottage that used to be inhabited by the local hangman stands here. Henchard comes here after he discovers that Elizabeth-Jane is not his daughter (Chapter 19), his sombre mood reflected in the natural background. Another melancholy background is Ten-Hatches-Hole, a weir where the river is deep and strong, and the noise of the water produces a *fugue of sounds*. This is the spot where Henchard is about to throw himself in the river when he sees his effigy floating in the water (Chapter 41).

The different social settings of the town are portrayed vividly. Henchard, the most prominent citizen, has one of the best houses. It is faced with red-and-grey old brick, and has a garden almost a quarter of a mile long (Chapter 9). Abel Whittle's home, on the other hand, is a little cottage in Back Street whose door is never locked because there is nothing valuable in the house. High-Place Hall, the house Lucetta moves into, is hard to categorize. It is *a great stone mansion* which has been empty for a year or so because its position overlooking the market-place has made it unpopular with potential occupiers. Lucetta decorates the house with *novel hangings and ingenious furniture* which she has gone to great trouble to instal. Henchard's reaction to Lucetta's stylish surroundings emphasizes Lucetta's foreignness in Casterbridge society.

The most disreputable area of Casterbridge is Mixen Lane. Although some honest and respectable families live here, it is mainly inhabited by unsavoury characters. The local inn looks respectable from the outside, but the front door is barred, the actual entrance being concealed in an alley. The seats in the inn are fastened by twine to hooks in the ceiling to keep them secure when the locals become boisterous.

Over to you

? Write a sentence for each theme to appear on a poster advertising the book.

? Make a Mind Map showing how characters and themes are connected.

? Test yourself by using the Mini Mind Map and the full Mind Map, as suggested at the start of this chapter.

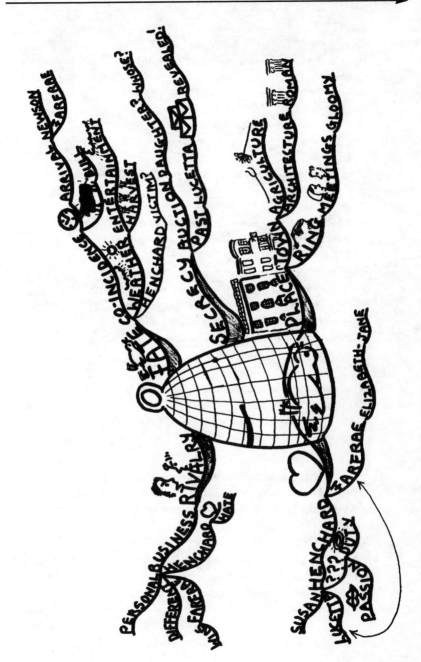

27

COMMENTARY

The Commentary looks at each chapter in turn, beginning with a brief preview which will prepare you for the chapter and help in last-minute revision. The Commentary comments on whatever is important in the chapter, focusing on the areas shown in the Mini Mind Map above.

ICONS

Wherever there is a focus on a particular theme, the icon for that theme appears in the margin (see p. x for key). Look out, too, for the 'Style and language' sections. Being able to comment on style and language will help you to get an 'A' in your exam.

You will learn more from the Commentary if you use it alongside the novel itself. Read a section from the novel, then the corresponding Commentary section – or the other way round.

QUESTIONS

Remember that when a question appears in the Commentary with a star ✪ in front of it, you should stop and think about it for a moment. And **do remember to take a break** after completing each exercise!

Ch. 1 *Susan is sold*

- Michael Henchard, his wife Susan and daughter Elizabeth-Jane approach Weydon Priors.
- A fair is in progress.
- They go into a furmity tent for refreshment.
- Henchard gets drunk.
- Henchard sells his wife and daughter to a sailor for five guineas.

Our first impression of the relationship between Henchard and Susan is one of *stale familiarity*. They do not seem happy together. They walk in silence and seem separate from each other. Although Henchard is a skilled hay-trusser and carries the tools of his trade, the couple are covered in dust and look shabby. They are searching for work and lodgings.

Henchard complains that he married too young and that his family is preventing him from succeeding in life. ❍ How does Susan react at first to Henchard's behaviour? Susan obeys Henchard's instruction to stand up, and bows her head with *absolute indifference* as she is sold. However, she gives Henchard a final warning not to touch the money, then throws her wedding ring in his face as she leaves with the sailor. ❍ What does this suggest about Susan's character?

Henchard is a fine figure with a *dogged and cynical personal indifference*. Although he realizes what he has done and has a *stolid look of concern* as Susan leaves, he decides not to go after her. ❍ Who do you sympathize with more at this stage – Henchard or Susan?

The sailor who buys Susan arrives at just the right moment. He speaks in a kindly way to Susan and says he will go through with the sale only if she is willing.

The furmity woman sets events in motion. Although the drink is non-alcoholic, she accepts payment to lace it with rum. She appears three more times in the story.

STYLE AND LANGUAGE

Images of nature reflect and comment on the action. The *weak bird* singing a *trite old evening song* suggests the staleness and tiredness of the pair's relationship. Look for more bird images as you read the story. The horses nuzzling each other lovingly remind us of the lack of love in the Henchard marriage. The horse auction in the field outside highlights the crude nature of the auction of Susan. Look for similar animal images as you read on.

Ch. 2 *The oath and the search*

◆ The next morning Henchard remembers what happened.
◆ Henchard swears an oath to give up alcohol.
◆ For months Henchard searches for his wife and daughter.
◆ Susan and Elizabeth-Jane have emigrated.
◆ Henchard decides to settle in Casterbridge.

The next morning Henchard experiences a variety of emotions. He is *surprised and nettled* that this time Susan took his behaviour seriously. He feels shame and deep regret. He is also concerned for his reputation, and is relieved that he hadn't revealed his name. His shame and determination to reform himself are shown by his solemn oath to avoid alcohol for 21 years – which he succeeds in doing. Henchard spends the sailor's money in the search for his wife and daughter, but doesn't want people to know the real circumstances of their disappearance. ○ How has your opinion and knowledge of Henchard changed?

Susan, according to Henchard, is placid and meek with *idiotic simplicity*. The *extreme simplicity of her intellect* would have made her believe that the auction had a binding force. ○ What do you think of this assessment of Susan's character? Look at the spirited way she throws her ring at Henchard, and the decisive way she tells him she would be better off trying her luck with someone else. Susan also looks closely at the sailor, as if recognizing his kindness and comparing it with Henchard's temper.

Ch. 3 *The return*

◆ Nineteen years later, Susan and Elizabeth-Jane approach Weydon Priors on fair day.
◆ They are in mourning for the sailor, Newson.

◆ Susan tells Elizabeth-Jane that Henchard is a distant relation.
◆ The furmity woman tells them that Henchard is in Casterbridge.

This journey to Weydon Priors is a contrast to the journey made 19 years earlier. Susan and Elizabeth-Jane walk hand in hand and behave affectionately towards each other. Susan has not told Elizabeth-Jane that she had been married to Henchard. This is the first example of the many incidents of secrecy and deception in the story.
○ What do you think about the way Susan keeps the history of her and Henchard a secret? What might her motives be?

Elizabeth-Jane doesn't want Susan to speak to the furmity woman because it's not respectable. She remarks that only the lowest people buy refreshment at the furmity tent. Elizabeth-Jane has strong ideas about the correct way to behave and we sense that she is ambitious to improve her station in life.

Hardy makes us aware of the passing of time and the changes in the rural way of life. Mechanical improvements have been made to some of the fairground machinery, but business at the centuries-old Weydon Priors Fair has dwindled. The furmity woman has few customers and is not prospering. Add to your notes on the furmity woman's appearances throughout the story.

Ch. 4 *From Canada to Casterbridge*

Flashback of the last 19 years:
◆ Susan and Elizabeth-Jane went to Canada with Newson.
◆ They returned, to Falmouth.
◆ A friend's comments made Susan doubt if her marriage to Newson was binding.
◆ Newson was reported lost at sea.

Present:
◆ Susan looks for Henchard to gain a better life for Elizabeth-Jane.
◆ They arrive in Casterbridge.
◆ People are complaining about a corn-factor who has sold bad wheat to the bakers.

Susan worked hard in Canada to maintain a pleasant home for her family. In her simplicity, she believed that Newson had a moral right to her. When she realizes that she is not legally married to Newson her conscience makes her feel she can't stay with him. The news of his death solves the problem for her. Susan recognizes Elizabeth-Jane's desire to better and improve herself, and decides to find Henchard and see if he can help. ○ What are the pros and cons of Susan's decision to find Henchard?

Elizabeth-Jane wants social advancement, but is also concerned to develop intellectually. She *sought further into things than other girls in her position ever did.*

Hardy gives us a clear impression of Casterbridge. We see an old town with ancient defences, a busy market-place and a church with a massive square tower where the bell tolls the signal for the end of the day's business. The town's business is agriculture, as can be seen by the objects on sale in the shop windows.

STYLE AND LANGUAGE
Hardy's training as an architect is evident in the detailed descriptions of places and buildings. Expressions such as *brick-nogging* (a timber framework filled with bricks) help to give a precise and vivid picture of the place. ○ What other examples of architectural terms can you find? Underline them as you go through the book.

Another feature of Hardy's style is the presentation of scenes shown through 'frames', such as windows or doorways. Casterbridge itself is 'framed' by gnarled trees.

The use of dialect (local way of speaking) makes the characters come alive. The woman complaining about the bread says it made *all the poor volks' insides plim* (swell) *like blowed bladders.* ○ What kind of characters speak the local dialect?

Ch. 5 *Meet the Mayor*

◆ Susan and Elizabeth-Jane see Henchard through the window of the King's Arms.
◆ Henchard is Mayor of Casterbridge and a successful corn merchant.
◆ Henchard bought the wheat that made the bad bread.

Henchard's appearance and clothes display his wealth and success and form a strong contrast with our last picture of him. He has kept his promise not to drink alcohol. ✪ What does this tell you about his character? Henchard shows signs of anger when he is asked about the bad bread, and says that he cannot turn grown (sprouted) wheat into wholesome wheat.

Susan had thought that Henchard might be dead, or in the workhouse. Now that she sees that he is rich and powerful, she is reluctant to approach him. ✪ Why might Susan feel like this? It is 19 years since the wife auction. Elizabeth-Jane was then a tiny girl; she is now 18 years old. ✪ What does this discrepancy suggest? Does it affect what you think about Susan's decision to find Henchard?

Test yourself

? Circle any words below that describe Henchard. Use another colour for any that describe Susan. Do the same for Elizabeth-Jane. Underline any words that apply to both Henchard and Susan.
cautious   impulsive   short-tempered   stupid
    patient   calculating   meek   simple   determined
clever   unselfish   placid   scheming   stable
    strong-minded   faithful   trustworthy

? Who said:
The little one too – the more the merrier! (Chapter 1)
Her present owner is not at all to her liking. (Chapter 1)
Meek – that meekness has done me more harm that the bitterest temper! (Chapter 2)
He's not a near relation, I suppose? (Chapter 3)
What an old-fashioned place it seems to be! (Chapter 4)

I have advertised for … a manager of the corn department. (Chapter 5)

? Mind Map your impressions so far of Henchard, Susan and Elizabeth-Jane. Add to your Mind Maps as you go through the book.

? Keep a record of the furmity woman's appearances. Record your observations about the significance of her appearance in the form of a Mind Map, or a chart.

Now you've seen Henchard climb back from the bottom to the top, take a break and prepare to meet someone who becomes a threat to his position!

Ch. 6 *Enter Farfrae*

◆ A young man hears Henchard's remarks about the corn.
◆ He writes Henchard a note.
◆ He gets lodgings at the Three Mariners.
◆ Susan and Elizabeth-Jane also get lodgings at the Three Mariners.

Our first impression of Donald Farfrae is that he is pleasant and instinctively wants to be helpful: he sends Henchard, a total stranger, some information about processing corn. Notice that he asks for a moderately priced hotel room. ✪ What might this suggest about his character?

Fate is bringing these characters together. Elizabeth-Jane has noticed Farfrae because of his Scottish accent and the note he sent to Henchard. She thinks the hotel recommended to Farfrae would be suitable for her and Susan. This is the beginning of Elizabeth-Jane's interest in Farfrae.

Ch. 7 *First meeting*

- Elizabeth-Jane works for the inn-keeper to help to pay for their accommodation.
- Farfrae tells Henchard about the process for restoring bad corn.
- Henchard offers Farfrae a job as corn manager.
- Susan overhears their conversation.
- Farfrae refuses because he is on his way to America.

Elizabeth-Jane shows resourcefulness and a practical nature as she helps out in the inn to reduce their bill. She feels that the Mariners is a *respectable* place to stay, and is willing to sacrifice her own comfort to enable herself and Susan to lodge there. Look at how Elizabeth-Jane takes in the details of Farfrae's appearance when she takes his supper to him.

Is it fate or coincidence that Farfrae happened to arrive in Casterbridge just as Henchard was advertising for a manager? Henchard is impressed by Farfrae's generosity in giving him the information without wanting payment, and also by Farfrae's scientific judgement and knowledge. Henchard says that he himself is a *rule o' thumb sort of man*. ✪ What do you think Henchard means by this? It is **ironic** (a word that describes an event whose significance isn't seen at the time) that Henchard begs Farfrae to take the manager's job, little suspecting that one day Farfrae will take his place as corn-factor and mayor. ✪ What does Henchard's immediate liking for Farfrae suggest about Henchard's character?

Susan overhears Henchard say that he has kept his oath not to drink. He took the oath because of something shameful that he did in his past. ✪ What might Susan think as she hears this?

Ch. 8 *Scottish songs*

- Farfrae sings Scottish songs with the drinkers at the Three Mariners.
- Elizabeth-Jane's good impression of Farfrae is increased.
- Henchard listens outside.

Farfrae's emotional singing makes him popular with the listeners. They are sorry to hear that he will not be staying in Casterbridge. Elizabeth-Jane likes Farfrae's thoughtful responses to the rustics' comments and feels that, like her, Farfrae sees life as essentially tragic and serious. She also thinks that, like her, he is more respectable than the rustics.

Christopher Coney and Solomon Longways are two of the minor rustic characters. Through their questions and comments we discover more about characters and events.

We see Henchard's loneliness as he listens on the other side of the window. He is a separate, isolated figure. Look at the way he is drawn towards Farfrae, the man who will later be his greatest rival. ❂ Which character do you sympathize more with at this point, Henchard or Farfrae?

Ch. 9 *The new corn-manager*

◆ Farfrae agrees to stay and be Henchard's corn manager.
◆ Susan sends Elizabeth-Jane to Henchard with a letter.
◆ Elizabeth-Jane is surprised to find Farfrae at Henchard's yard.

Henchard employs Farfrae from business and emotional motives. Henchard, a man of *strong impulses* is delighted when Farfrae accepts the position of corn manager and agrees to take temporary lodgings in Henchard's house. Farfrae can name his own terms for the job. Henchard is confident and warm towards his new *friend*. ❂ What do you think about Henchard's judgement?

Elizabeth-Jane feels hurt that Farfrae didn't say goodbye to her. ❂ What do you think she feels when she sees Farfrae at Henchard's offices?

Ch. 10 *News for Jopp and for Henchard*

◆ Joshua Jopp is told that a corn manager has already been appointed.
◆ Henchard writes a note back to Susan.
◆ Henchard encloses five guineas in the note.
◆ Henchard asks Susan to meet him at the Ring.

Jopp is angry and disappointed to hear that he is not the new manager. ✪ What do you think of Henchard's behaviour to Jopp? Is he being fair?

Henchard treats Elizabeth-Jane with warmth and delicacy, in contrast to the way he behaves towards Jopp. His first reaction to the news of Susan's reappearance is one of relief that Susan hasn't told anyone, including Elizabeth-Jane, about his past actions. Henchard is moved by his meeting with Elizabeth-Jane, and realizes that she and Susan are quite poor. Notice how Henchard is about to send Susan five pounds, then increases the sum to five guineas. ✪ Why does Henchard send this particular amount of money? What message will it give to Susan?

Henchard suddenly thinks that the two women might be impostors, but he is reassured by *something* in Elizabeth-Jane that she is his daughter. ✪ Why is this ironic? Notice that his interest in Farfrae is eclipsed by this new development, causing Farfrae to wonder at Henchard's sudden changes of mood.

STYLE AND LANGUAGE

An effective feature of Hardy's style is the use of incidents and references that parallel and echo each other. This device helps to make us more intensely aware of the workings of fate and destiny in the novel, and also helps to reveal aspects of character and plot. In this chapter, the sum of five guineas that Henchard sends to Susan balances the sum of five guineas for which he earlier sold her, and makes us see Henchard's guilt and remorse for what he had done. Elizabeth-Jane's eyes in this chapter are described as *aerial-grey*; in Chapter 1 they were *black*. This pairing of descriptions intensifies the irony of Henchard's belief that his daughter has returned. ✪ Look out for more examples of paired incidents as you read the novel.

Memory work-out

? What important events take place in each of these inns?

? Who:
  – wore an *old-fashioned evening suit*? (Chapter 5)
  – was a *young man of remarkably pleasant aspect*? (Chapter 6)
  – was at his wits' end about bad wheat? (Chapter 7)
  – worked as a waitress? (Chapter 8)
  – listened outside a window? (Chapter 8)
  – got a job as a corn manager? (Chapter 9)
  – wrote to Henchard? (two people: Chapter 6, Chapter 9)
  – didn't get a job as a corn manager? (Chapter 10)

? Begin a Mind Map of your impressions of Donald Farfrae. Add to it as you go through the book.

Now you've seen Henchard overwhelmed by all he has gained in the course of a day, take a break before a dramatic meeting.

Ch. 11 *Henchard and Susan meet*

◆ Description of the Ring, the Roman ampitheatre.
◆ Henchard meets Susan.
◆ Henchard suggests a plan: he will court and remarry Susan.

The description of the Ring evokes a huge circular enclosure, an impressive Roman remain associated with gruesome and tragic spectacles. The reference to skeletons dug up in the area highlights the idea that a skeleton from Henchard's past is about to confront him. The gloomy atmosphere of the background for Henchard's meeting with Susan suggests that the eventual outcome will not be happy.

The meeting between Henchard and Susan is emotional. He supports her in his arms, and his first words are to tell her that he hasn't drunk since the day of the auction. ❍ What kind of music would you choose to accompany this scene on a film?

Both Henchard and Susan want to keep secrets. Henchard's plan will make it seem as if he has just met Susan. He doesn't want Elizabeth-Jane to know the truth, and he doesn't want the town to know about his *shady, headstrong, disgraceful life as a young man.* Susan is practising a double deception – she is also deceiving Henchard about Elizabeth-Jane. Susan says she is doing everything for the sake of Elizabeth-Jane. ❍ Do you think she is justified in deceiving Henchard? Do you think she has forgiven Henchard? Should she forgive him?

STYLE AND LANGUAGE

Hardy's language creates an effective description of the Ring and its sombre atmosphere. The simile describing how people sitting there dozing or reading would look at the slopes *as if watching the gladiatorial combat* brings the area's bloodthirsty past alive. The description of the arena overgrown with grass that *was bearded with withered bents that formed waves under the brush of the wind* creates a melancholy picture. Notice how **alliteration** adds to the vividness of the sentence. (Alliteration is the repetition of a sound at the beginnings of words.)

Ch. 12 *A woman in Jersey*

◆ Henchard tells Farfrae that the wife and daughter he separated from 19 years ago have returned.
◆ Henchard tells Farfrae that he plans to remarry Susan.
◆ Elizabeth-Jane must not know the truth.
◆ A complication – Henchard has promised to marry a woman in Jersey.
◆ Farfrae drafts a letter of explanation for Henchard to send to the woman.

Farfrae is working late, sorting out Henchard's accounts. There is a strong contrast between Farfrae's efficiency and Henchard's more traditional hit-and-miss approach and dislike of paperwork. Farfrae is a good judge of character – he recognizes Henchard's impulsive, extreme nature and likes his warmth, even if these characteristics can make Henchard difficult to deal with. ❂ What do you see as the main differences between Henchard and Farfrae?

We see Henchard's loneliness as he confides in Farfrae, whom he barely knows, because he has no-one else to talk to. ❂ What detail of his parting from Susan does he not tell Farfrae? Why does he keep quiet about this? Henchard takes responsibility for the mistakes he has made, in selling Susan and in selfishly letting the woman in Jersey become devoted to him. He wants to make amends to both women, and shows principle in saying that his first duty is to Susan. Henchard is troubled in his mind, although he is rich and successful.

Farfrae says that Henchard should tell the truth to Elizabeth-Jane. ❂ What do you think?

Ch. 13 *The remarriage*

◆ Henchard rents a cottage for Susan and Elizabeth-Jane.
◆ After a few months' courtship, Henchard and Susan remarry.

Henchard courts Susan with *business-like determination*. He is motivated by his sense of what is right rather than by emotion. His intentions are to make amends to Susan, to give Elizabeth-

Jane a comfortable home and to punish himself for his past wrongdoings. One aspect of the punishment is that people will think less of him for marrying a humble woman, who is nicknamed 'The Ghost' because of her pallor. ✪ Is there any love in the marriage?

The rustics are unimpressed by the marriage. They do not understand why Henchard is marrying such a *poor fragile woman*. There is some joking that Susan, *a mere skellinton*, has found another husband, giving hope for Nance Mockridge and Mother Cuxsom.

Henchard's confidence in Farfrae grows. We sense the irony as he says that soon he will be able to leave everything to Farfrae. Farfrae, of course, ends up with a great deal that belonged to Henchard, against Henchard's will.

Ch. 14 *Meeting at the granary*

◆ Susan and Elizabeth-Jane lead more comfortable, affluent lives.
◆ Henchard wants to adopt Elizabeth-Jane and change her name to his.
◆ Susan opposes this plan.
◆ Elizabeth-Jane and Farfrae are tricked into meeting at an empty granary.

Elizabeth-Jane's new way of life enables her to develop. However, she remembers her life of poverty and is not self-indulgent, dressing in a sensible and restrained way and not spending money unnecessarily.

Henchard has become very fond of Elizabeth-Jane. We see Henchard through Elizabeth-Jane's eyes; her viewpoint is the same as Hardy's. Through Elizabeth-Jane's *great natural insight* we see Henchard's growing affection and continued admiration for Farfrae, and his tendency to domineer. Henchard's business thrives under Farfrae's modern methods, although the *rugged picturesqueness* of the old way disappears.

Susan doesn't want Elizabeth-Jane to be called Henchard, and she is uneasy when Henchard comments on Elizabeth-Jane's changed hair colour. ✪ Why does Susan react in this way? Look at how she persuades Elizabeth-Jane that it would be wrong to change her name. ❍ Do you think that *simple* is an adequate description of Susan? Who writes the note to make Farfrae and Elizabeth-Jane meet at the granary?

Farfrae and Elizabeth-Jane seem calm when they realize that they have been tricked. ❍ Can you see any signs that they might be interested in each other?

Ch. 15 *Abel's breeches*

◆ Elizabeth-Jane is admired for her attractive appearance.
◆ Henchard and Farfrae quarrel over the treatment of Abel Whittle.
◆ Farfrae gains popularity because of his expertise and personality.
◆ Henchard regrets having confided in Farfrae.

Elizabeth-Jane's dress sense and *budding beauty* bring her to people's attention, but she feels that her appearance masks her real self. Elizabeth-Jane continues to show a desire for learning and education.

Henchard's treatment of Abel Whittle, forcing him out to work without his trousers, is harsh and insensitive. ❍ What information are we given about Henchard's treatment of Abel's mother? How does this affect your opinion of Henchard's behaviour? Farfrae overrules Henchard's order, and his considerate way of managing gains him respect as Henchard loses it. Although the two men's friendship continues, Henchard thinks of Farfrae with a *dim dread*. Farfrae is becoming a rival for Henchard's focal position in the town.

Ch. 16 *Rival entertainments*

◆ Henchard and Farfrae organize entertainments.
◆ Henchard's entertainment fails: Farfrae's is a great success.
◆ Henchard says that Farfrae is going to leave him.
◆ Farfrae accepts Henchard's hint.

Farfrae's entertainment is under cover – he has borrowed waterproof cloths from Henchard. A spot in the Walks is transformed into a ballroom for dancing to a string band.

There is an admission charge. Henchard's entertainment consists of more traditional games and country activities. There is no admission fee, and a mammoth tea is provided free of charge. ❂ What do these different arrangements tell you about the men's different characters?

Fate works against Henchard as bad weather wrecks his show. Henchard had been sure that the fine weather would continue. ❂ How much do you think he is to blame for the failure of his entertainment? Might the local people in any case have chosen to go to Farfrae's instead?

We see Henchard as an outsider, jealous of Farfrae's success and popularity. ❂ Why does he dismiss Farfrae? What earlier event does this action remind you of?

Ch. 17 *Character is fate*

◆ Farfrae almost proposes to Elizabeth-Jane.
◆ Elizabeth-Jane realizes she is in love with Farfrae.
◆ Farfrae sets up in business on his own.
◆ Henchard forbids Farfrae to see Elizabeth-Jane.

Farfrae suggests that if he were richer and if Henchard weren't opposed to it, he would ask Elizabeth-Jane to marry him. When he receives Henchard's note, he decides to stop paying attention to Elizabeth-Jane, and stifles his considerable interest in her. ❂ What does this tell you about Farfrae's character?

Farfrae acts fairly towards Henchard. He shows a sense of honour when he refuses to take any of Henchard's trade. Later, though, Farfrae is forced into commercial competition with Henchard. Farfrae tries to be friendly to Henchard, but Henchard is angry and bitter, and refuses to acknowledge him.

Elizabeth-Jane realizes that she loves Farfrae but is unsure about his feelings towards her. She lacks confidence and feels that, although she is pretty, her inner self is not attractive or appealing.

Henchard is an increasingly isolated figure as his support in the town fades away. His rashness, jealousy and quick temper lead him into actions which bring him misery. Hardy reminds us of the saying *Character is Fate*. ❂ How far do you think this idea applies to *The Mayor of Casterbridge*? To what extent are Henchard's failure and Farfrae's success caused by their own characters, rather than chance?

STYLE AND LANGUAGE

Hardy compares Henchard with Bellerophon, a character from a Greek **myth**. (A myth, in the literary sense, is an old story, usually involving gods and human beings, which often contains hidden meanings.) The gods at first helped Bellerophon to overcome great obstacles and to achieve great success, but then the gods turned against him. He was inflicted by hardships and tragedies and became a lonely wanderer, grief-stricken and bitter. The comparison gives Henchard's story a universal significance and suggests that great suffering lies ahead of him.

Over to you

? From what you have seen so far, circle in one colour any words that apply to Henchard. Circle in another colour any that apply to Farfrae. Underline any words that apply to both.

> jealous   considerate   forceful   principled   fair
> thoughtless   careful   emotional   bears grudges
> generous   vulnerable   cautious   faithful
> strong   artistic   knowledgeable   persuasive

? Write one or more sentences that might be spoken about Henchard by (1) Elizabeth-Jane (2) Farfrae (3) Abel Whittle.

? Which characters are associated with the items of clothing shown in the illustration opposite? Give a brief explanation of the **context** in which they appear.

? Remember to add to your Mind Maps.

Can things get worse for Henchard? Take a short break and prepare for a blast from the past!

Ch. 18 *Letters and a death*

◆ Henchard receives a letter from his old love, Lucetta.
◆ Lucetta asks Henchard to meet her and return the love letters she sent him.
◆ Susan writes a letter to Henchard, not to be opened until Elizabeth-Jane's wedding day.
◆ Susan confesses that she had set up the meeting between Farfrae and Elizabeth-Jane.
◆ Susan dies.

Lucetta's letter brings another element of Henchard's past back into his life. Just as Susan and Elizabeth-Jane returned, causing Henchard to do the *right thing*, now Lucetta's renewed presence makes Henchard think that he *ought* to marry her if he could. Notice that Lucetta does not blame Henchard. She acknowledges that he was honest with her about his position, and she trusts him to keep their previous relationship secret. However, Henchard blames himself for causing Lucetta pain. ✪ Do you think that Henchard should marry Lucetta, now that Susan is dead? Why does Hardy make Susan die at this particular point?

The letters written by Lucetta and Susan's sealed note both contain secrets. By chance, Lucetta doesn't meet Henchard at the appointed time, leaving him still in possession of the revealing letters.

Susan engineered the meeting between Elizabeth-Jane and Farfrae because she wanted them to get married. Although she may be seen as a weak character, Susan does act to get what she wants. Elizabeth-Jane is socially and economically secure in Henchard's house, and eventually she does marry Farfrae. However, Susan's final request is not met. She wants her eyes to be closed with pennies when she dies, a superstitious practice thought to prevent the dead from becoming a ghost, and the pennies to be buried afterwards. Christopher Coney digs them up and spends them on beer. ✪ Look at the rustics' comments on his action, at the end of the chapter. What would you say if you were there?

Ch. 19 *Elizabeth-Jane's father*

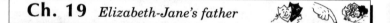

♦ Henchard tells Elizabeth-Jane that he is her real father.
♦ Henchard finds and reads Susan's letter.
♦ He discovers that his child died and that Elizabeth-Jane is Newson's daughter.
♦ Henchard keeps this fact a secret.
♦ Elizabeth-Jane accepts Henchard as her father.

Henchard's isolation is increased by Susan's death. He cannot resist trying to become closer to Elizabeth-Jane by telling her that he is her father. Henchard follows the craving of his heart to re-establish his tie with his daughter. We see that he is pleased when he wins his point and persuades Elizabeth-Jane to take his name, but his satisfaction is softened by tenderness. ✪ Who does Henchard have most feeling for – Susan, Elizabeth-Jane, or Lucetta?

Henchard comes across Susan's letter when searching for documentary proof of Elizabeth-Jane's parentage. Ironically, he finds that Newson, not he, is her father. ✪ Is it fate, or character, that brings about this discovery? Or both? The letter is not sealed properly, but is clearly marked. ✪ What choices does Henchard have when he finds the letter?

The dramatic timing of this discovery increases our perception of Henchard as a victim. He feels that some sinister power is punishing him. His loneliness and misery are intense. The gloomy river bank with its reminders of executions reflects the darkness in his heart.

STYLE AND LANGUAGE

Henchard's despondent mood is conveyed through phrases such as *voice of desolation, mournful phases* and *torturing cramps*. The final note of despair is struck with the last words of the chapter as Henchard sees the result of his remarriage to Susan as *dust and ashes*.

Ch. 20 *Elizabeth-Jane meets Lucetta*

◆ Henchard becomes critical of Elizabeth-Jane.
◆ Elizabeth-Jane meets Lucetta, who asks Elizabeth-Jane to live in her house as a companion.
◆ Henchard will not be invited to become an alderman – but Farfrae will.
◆ Henchard withdraws his objection to Farfrae seeing Elizabeth-Jane.

Henchard finds fault with aspects of Elizabeth-Jane's behaviour. He criticizes her use of dialect words, her handwriting and her willingness to perform manual and menial tasks. ❂ Why does Henchard behave like this? He is particularly angry when he finds out that Elizabeth-Jane worked at the Three Mariners and had served Farfrae.

Henchard's bitterness is increased when he discovers that Farfrae and not himself will become an alderman. He gives Farfrae permission to court Elizabeth-Jane because he wants to be rid of Newson's child. ❂ What do you think about the way Henchard treats Elizabeth-Jane?

Elizabeth-Jane is very aware of her lack of formal education and tries to improve herself through reading and studying. She is aware of Henchard's dislike of her, and is hurt by his cold treatment, but doesn't know what has caused his hostility. Elizabeth-Jane is delighted when Lucetta (as the young woman turns out to be) offers her a way out of an unbearable situation. She also hopes that if she becomes independent Henchard may grow to love her.

STYLE AND LANGUAGE

This chapter gives us another example of incidents that parallel each other. Henchard told his story to a stranger, Farfrae, and here Elizabeth-Jane confides in a stranger, Lucetta. Farfrae becomes Henchard's rival in business; Lucetta becomes Elizabeth-Jane's rival in love.

Ch. 21 *Moving out*

- ◆ Elizabeth goes to look at High-Place Hall.
- ◆ Henchard also visits the house.
- ◆ Henchard agrees that Elizabeth-Jane should move out.
- ◆ Henchard changes his mind and asks her to stay.

Henchard is indifferent to Elizabeth-Jane's plans to move out. He offers her an allowance, and seems relieved to get her off his hands. ○ Why does he offer her money? To which other two characters has Henchard given money? Henchard's attitude changes when he sees Elizabeth-Jane's room and realizes the attempts she has been making to improve herself. He asks her to stay, and says he will explain what has caused his behaviour towards her. Here we see another example of Henchard regretting an impulsive action, too late.

Lucetta is concerned that Elizabeth-Jane has not told her father where she is moving to; Henchard is shocked when he does hear her new address. He realizes that Lucetta and Miss Templeman are the same person. ○ Why has Lucetta asked Elizabeth-Jane to live in her house? What do you think about her plan?

STYLE AND LANGUAGE

The architecture of Lucetta's house is described, with particular reference to an old arched and studded door, whose keystone is in the shape of a mask. The mask is chipped and has an unpleasant appearance. The mask and the tucked-away position of the hall suggest intrigue, and may reflect something of Lucetta's colourful and somewhat shady character.

Ch. 22 *More letters from Lucetta*

◆ Henchard's presence the night before is explained.
◆ Lucetta had written, saying she had moved to Casterbridge and suggesting marriage.
◆ Lucetta writes again but Henchard delays visiting.
◆ Lucetta gets rid of Elizabeth-Jane.
◆ Lucetta receives a visitor.

Henchard is interested to receive Lucetta's letter and suggestion of marriage. His discovery that Elizabeth-Jane is not his child has left an *emotional void* that he longs to fill. However, you may notice that he does not feel passionately about Lucetta, and the knowledge that Lucetta is now rich adds to her charm. Henchard is motivated by what he feels is the right thing to do. ❂ On what other occasion did Henchard make a decision based on a sense of duty?

Lucetta's plan to use Elizabeth-Jane to give Henchard an excuse for visiting her is artful and calculating. She has also calculated the advantages of marrying Henchard; she wants to wipe out any lack of respectability in her past and to secure her new social position. Lucetta's plan is thwarted when she realizes that the quarrel between Elizabeth-Jane and Henchard may prevent him from visiting, so she acts quickly and sends the girl out for the morning. ❂ What are your feelings for Elizabeth-Jane at this point? When Lucetta is waiting for her visitor, she tries out different poses to find the one that will make her seem most attractive, adding to our impression of her shallowness and artificiality. Lucetta is timid and nervous while waiting and hides when the visitor arrives. She seems rather unstable and easily upset. Tension is created when we are told that the visitor is not Henchard.

The description of the market-day activities adds to the picture of Casterbridge. References to the open square with its jostling people and crossing vehicles and details of what was worn and carried – *leggings, switches, sample books* – build a lively scene.

Recap and recall

? Begin a Mind Map of Lucetta.

? What is your final assessment of Susan? Make some notes or a Mini Mind Map to support your view.

? Put these extracts from notes and letters in the order in which they appear in the story. Say who wrote each one.

I have therefore sent her away for the morning.

Meet me at eight o'clock this evening, if you can, at the Ring on the Budmouth Road.

It is for your good and mine, as I hope, that I have come to live at Casterbridge.

I therefore withdraw my objection.

Elizabeth-Jane is not your Elizabeth-Jane.

You probably are aware of my arrangement with your daughter.

I make request henceforth that you and my stepdaughter be as strangers to each other.

Now take a break before meeting the unexpected visitor.

Ch. 23 *Lucetta and Farfrae meet*

◆ The visitor is Farfrae, come to court Elizabeth-Jane.
◆ Lucetta is attracted to him.
◆ Farfrae prevents the parting of two lovers by employing the young man and his father.
◆ Lucetta refuses to see Henchard.

Farfrae has made a profitable business transaction and is in a position to marry. Elizabeth-Jane seems a good choice, being *pleasing, thrifty and satisfactory*. Marriage to her would also lead to reconciliation with Henchard. ○ What do you think of Farfrae's reasons for marrying Elizabeth-Jane? What are her feelings for him?

Lucetta and Farfrae are interested in and attracted to each other. At the hiring fair Lucetta is delighted with the way Farfrae enables two lovers to stay together by hiring both the young man and his father. Both Farfrae and Lucetta are moved to tears at the thought of the young pair having to part. ❂ In what ways are Farfrae and Lucetta similar? Lucetta asks Farfrae not to listen to gossip about her. ❂ How likely is it that Lucetta will be able to keep her past a secret?

Lucetta had planned to use Elizabeth-Jane to bring Henchard to the house; now she plans to use Elizabeth-Jane's presence to keep Henchard away! ❂ Can you think of any character who is genuinely interested in Elizabeth-Jane's welfare?

Ch. 24 *Market-day*

◆ Elizabeth-Jane and Lucetta are interested in Farfrae.
◆ Farfrae introduces a revolutionary new seed-planting machine to Casterbridge.
◆ Lucetta tells Elizabeth-Jane about a woman who meets a man she prefers to the man she is promised to.
◆ Elizabeth-Jane guesses that Lucetta is talking about herself.

Elizabeth-Jane doesn't know that Farfrae is attracted to Lucetta. She and Lucetta long for market-day when they will see Farfrae through the window. The difference between the restrained Elizabeth-Jane and the flamboyant Lucetta is seen in the seriousness with which Lucetta chooses which dress to buy. Lucetta suggests that her personality changes according to what she wears. Lucetta's changeable nature emphasizes Elizabeth-Jane's firm and steady character.

The new machine, a horse-drawn implement for sowing the seed, causes a sensation. ❂ Where has there been an earlier example of Farfrae's knowledge of up-to-date methods? Elizabeth-Jane accepts that the change will be more efficient, but at the same time regrets the passing of the old way. Henchard is scornfully dismissive of the machine. Although he prefers the old, traditional farming methods, he has admired Farfrae's knowledge of new techniques. ❂ What causes Henchard to ridicule the machine and the person who recommended it?

Elizabeth-Jane is observant and reflective, and notices the attraction between Lucetta and Farfrae, and how they try to conceal it. However, although she guesses that the woman in Lucetta's story is Lucetta herself, she doesn't realize that the two men involved are her stepfather and the man she loves.

Ch. 25 *Rivals in love*

♦ Farfrae visits Lucetta and ignores Elizabeth-Jane.
♦ Henchard proposes to Lucetta.
♦ Lucetta doesn't give an answer.

Farfrae is drawn by Lucetta's liveliness and variety, and is no longer interested in Elizabeth-Jane. ❂ Who does Hardy want us to see as the better woman – Lucetta or Elizabeth-Jane? What does Farfrae's attraction to Lucetta suggest to you about his character?

Henchard's feelings for Lucetta become stronger as she seems inaccessible. Lucetta has the upper hand in their relationship now, Henchard appearing awkward and unsophisticated in her fashionable drawing room. He is aware that he lacks the polish that Lucetta has recently acquired, and is stung into arguing with her. Henchard regards Lucetta as *almost his property*. ❂ Which other of his relationships does this phrase remind you of?

Elizabeth-Jane accepts stoically Farfrae's lack of interest in her and his relationship with Lucetta. She is hurt by the way that Farfrae and Henchard ignore her, but finds some amusement in watching them fawn on Lucetta. Elizabeth-Jane's clear and analytical mind enables her to recognize that Farfrae is *desperately enamoured of* Lucetta, while Henchard's emotion is the *artificially stimulated coveting of maturer age*. Elizabeth-Jane is used to renunciation and disappointment. However, although she is accustomed to *the wreck of each day's wishes*, she feels that she will be granted something in place of what she has lost.

Ch. 26 *Hiring and firing*

♦ Henchard suspects that Farfrae is his rival for Lucetta.
♦ Henchard hires Jopp to manage his business and provide competition for Farfrae.
♦ Henchard buys up grain, following a weather-prophet's prediction of a poor harvest.
♦ The harvest looks good; Henchard sells at a loss.
♦ Henchard dismisses Jopp.

Henchard is very slow to gather that Farfrae is his rival for Lucetta. Similarly, Farfrae does not realize that Lucetta is the woman Henchard is talking about. They are both so wrapped up in their own thoughts and feelings that they are unaware even of situations that will affect them deeply. Elizabeth-Jane highlights the absurdity of the scene where Lucetta and the two men have tea together with her comment: *'How ridiculous of all three of them!'*

❂ Which one do you think Lucetta should marry? What about Elizabeth-Jane? At this point, do you hope that Farfrae will get over Lucetta and turn to Elizabeth-Jane, as he had intended?

Henchard hires Jopp to drive Farfrae out of business by hard but fair competition. The rivalry in love has sharpened the business rivalry. ❂ What reason does Jopp have for disliking Farfrae? Notice that Jopp knows that Lucetta came from Jersey.

Henchard doesn't take in the fact that Jopp may know something of his and Lucetta's past. Jopp is also not the right man for the job, as Elizabeth-Jane tries to point out. ❂ How would you describe Henchard's decision to hire Jopp? What does Elizabeth-Jane's accurate assessment of Jopp tell you about her character? What do you think about the way she tells Henchard that he's making a mistake?

Henchard's decision to consult Fall the weather-prophet to confirm his own prediction shows his superstitious nature. Such consultations (although everyone pretended not to believe the forecasts) were common in a town which depended on the success of the wheat crop. Hardy vividly depicts the tension among the farmers as they try to predict what the weather will be like in August.

Jopp now has more reason to dislike Farfrae, this being the second time that Farfrae's success has caused him to lose a job. He also has reason to dislike Henchard.

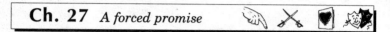

Ch. 27 *A forced promise*

- ◆ The good weather gives way to bad, as the forecaster had predicted.
- ◆ The rivalry between Henchard and Farfrae is taken up by their men.
- ◆ Henchard overhears Lucetta and Farfrae talk of their love for each other.
- ◆ Henchard forces Lucetta to promise to marry him, with Elizabeth-Jane as witness.

Henchard might have avoided losing such vast amounts of money if he had waited long enough before selling all the corn he had bought – but patience is not in Henchard's nature. He experiences moody depression, and wonders if fate is working against him. The fight between Henchard's and Farfrae's waggoners parallels and **foreshadows** the later fight between the two men.

Henchard is agitated by the conversation he overhears, and anxious to secure Lucetta, forces her into a promise of marriage by threatening to reveal her past. Notice that it is the thought that Farfrae is his rival that makes him merciless in this.
❂ Do you sympathize with Henchard here? Elizabeth-Jane sees Henchard's harsh treatment of Lucetta, and she sees Lucetta's distress and misery. Elizabeth-Jane realizes that there is a secret relationship between Henchard and Lucetta: *'Ah – you have many many secrets from me!'* ❂ Which characters in the novel are affected by secrets and deceitful actions?

Ch. 28 *Henchard's secret revealed*

- ◆ Henchard presides at the magistrate's court.
- ◆ The furmity woman appears, charged with disorderly conduct.
- ◆ The furmity woman reveals Henchard's past.
- ◆ Lucetta goes away to Port-Bredy for a few days.

Henchard is no longer the Mayor, but as a magistrate, he has to deal fairly with the people who appear before him. His *rough and ready perceptions* and his *sledge-hammer directness* enable him to perform this role successfully. ❂ How fairly does Henchard treat people in his private life?

Henchard doesn't deny what the furmity woman says. ❂ Could he have denied her story? Why doesn't he? Fate has caused Henchard to stand in as a magistrate on the very day that the furmity woman is brought to court. His past has caught up with him and his greatest secret is now common knowledge. ❂ Can anything go right for Henchard now?

Ch. 29 *A rescue and a revelation*

◆ Lucetta and Elizabeth-Jane meet on the Port-Bredy road.
◆ A bull attacks the two women.
◆ Henchard saves them.
◆ Lucetta has married Farfrae.

Lucetta's restlessness and odd behaviour in walking back along the road she has so recently left suggest that she has something to hide. Henchard acts bravely in tackling the bull, his roughness and aggression being welcome in this circumstance. He is tender and gentle with the women – although he takes particular care of Lucetta, little knowing that she has just married Farfrae. ❂ What are your feelings for Henchard here?

Henchard asks Lucetta to help him by telling Gower, a man to whom Henchard owes money, that they will be married in the next couple of weeks, so giving him time to pay. Ironically Gower was the witness to the marriage between Farfrae and Lucetta. An additional irony for Henchard is that he has just saved his rival's wife. Lucetta says that she married Farfrae because she was scared that Henchard would tell him of her past; she also felt she could not marry Henchard now she heard about his past. ❂ Lucetta has married Farfrae although she had promised to marry Henchard. What do you think of the reasons she gives? Is her action justified?

Gather your thoughts

?   Add to your comments on the furmity woman's appearances.

?   Look at the list of events in Henchard's life, below. Decide how far his *character* contributes to the circumstances of each event, and how far *fate* acts against him. Mark each event with C or F or both.

- Newson arrives just at the right moment to buy Susan and Elizabeth-Jane.
- Henchard appoints Farfrae.
- Henchard first rejects, then later dismisses Jopp.
- Henchard's celebrations are ruined by rain.
- Henchard dismisses Farfrae.
- Henchard opens and reads Susan's letter.
- Lucetta comes to live in Casterbridge.
- Henchard loses all his money buying up grain and selling at a loss.
- The furmity woman reveals Henchard's secret.
- Lucetta marries Farfrae.

?   What advice would you give Lucetta about what she should do?

Now that you've seen Henchard lose and Farfrae win yet again, take time out before seeing how Elizabeth-Jane will cope with the new situation.

Ch. 30 *Moving out again*

◆ Lucetta tells Elizabeth-Jane about her marriage.
◆ Elizabeth-Jane is shocked and moves out.

At first Elizabeth-Jane thinks that Lucetta has married Henchard, so her shock and distress are all the greater when she realizes the truth. Elizabeth-Jane feels that she cannot continue to live in the house with Farfrae and Lucetta. Her sense of respectability and her craving for correct behaviour make it impossible for her to stay at High-Place Hall. Also, she cannot stay in the same house as Farfrae, *so nearly her avowed lover.* ✪ Do you understand Elizabeth-Jane's strong desire for respectability? What has caused it?

Lucetta is entirely absorbed in her own affairs and accepts Elizabeth-Jane's departure from the house. She has married Farfrae without telling him of her past, and feels some uneasiness when she thinks of Henchard. ✪ What do you think of Lucetta's treatment of Elizabeth-Jane? Should Elizabeth-Jane have made clear her own interest in Farfrae?

Ch. 31 *The final downfall*

◆ Henchard is bankrupt.
◆ Henchard goes to live in Jopp's cottage.
◆ Farfrae takes over Henchard's business.

Henchard's descent begins when the story of his past becomes common knowledge. Other events contribute to his downfall: someone who owes him a lot of money is unable to pay, and one of his workers lowers Henchard's reputation by false representation of the quality of some corn.

Henchard's behaviour is honourable. He hides nothing and makes every attempt to be fair, even selling his gold watch to pay one of his poor creditors. Henchard has to leave his home and take up lodgings with Jopp in Mixen Lane, a slum area of the town. Henchard's self-esteem is so low that he can live only with the one man in Casterbridge whose opinion means nothing to him. He is an isolated figure, refusing all visitors, even Elizabeth-Jane.

We learn from Abel Whittle that Farfrae is a popular master even though he pays less than Henchard did. ✪ What did the men dislike about Henchard's way of working? More scientific farming methods are being used, replacing the old *guesswork.* We are made aware of the differences between Farfrae and Henchard and of the changes in agricultural working practices.

STYLE AND LANGUAGE

This chapter provides one of the most poignant 'pairings' in the novel. The auction of all Henchard's possessions echoes the earlier auction of Susan, which resulted in Henchard creating a *position of affluence out of absolutely nothing*. Once again he is left with absolutely nothing, but this time the sense of despair is so profound that we doubt if he will be able to overcome it.

Ch. 32 *Farfrae has it all*

◆ Farfrae has moved into Henchard's house and bought his furniture.
◆ Farfrae offers Henchard rooms in his old house, and what furniture he would like.
◆ Henchard is ill and is nursed by Elizabeth-Jane.
◆ Henchard gets employment as a hay-trusser with Farfrae.
◆ Henchard's vow of abstinence from drink comes to its end.

Jopp tells Henchard that Farfrae is living in his house and has bought his furniture. ❂ What do you think Jopp feels as he gives Henchard this news? Henchard is moved by Farfrae's generous offers of accommodation, furniture, a meal: *'I sometimes think I've wronged 'ee.'* ❂ What did Henchard offer Farfrae when they first met? Has Farfrae discussed the matter of accommodation with Lucetta? How would Lucetta react to the suggestion?

Farfrae now has Henchard's business, his house and his furniture. He is likely to be mayor, is married to the woman Henchard wanted to marry and is Henchard's employer. Henchard, *the once flourishing merchant and mayor*, now works as a labourer in the business he once owned. ❂ How sensitive is Farfrae to the change in their positions?

The one thing Henchard still has is Elizabeth-Jane's love and loyalty. ❂ How important is it that Henchard should not lose her affection?

Ch. 33 *Henchard drinks again*

- ◆ Henchard drinks in the Three Mariners.
- ◆ He asks the choir to sing a psalm as a threat to Farfrae.
- ◆ Lucetta writes a note to Henchard.
- ◆ Elizabeth-Jane fears that Henchard may harm Farfrae.

Henchard ends his 21 years of abstinence by joining the journeymen for their customary drink after Sunday church. This scene brings to mind the earlier time when Farfrae sang in the Three Mariners. ❂ How is the atmosphere different on this occasion?

Henchard is very sarcastic to Lucetta when she sees him in Farfrae's yard. ❂ Why does Henchard behave in this way? What is he feeling? Lucetta writes to him about his behaviour, apparently not realizing that Henchard could show the note to Farfrae. Lucetta's addiction to writing letters means that there is plenty of incriminating evidence about the past she wishes to hide. However, Henchard destroys the note, even though it gives him an opportunity to hit back at Farfrae.

Also, although Elizabeth-Jane is alarmed by Henchard's expression and gesture when Farfrae is standing dangerously near a trapdoor, Henchard doesn't actually harm Farfrae. ❂ Do you think Henchard is a bad man? What are his major faults? What makes you sympathize with him?

Ch. 34 *More about Lucetta's letters*

- ◆ Elizabeth-Jane and others warn Farfrae of Henchard's hatred.
- ◆ Farfrae changes his mind about setting up Henchard with a seedshop.
- ◆ Lucetta asks Henchard to return her letters.
- ◆ Henchard reads extracts from the letters to Farfrae, but doesn't disclose Lucetta's name.

Farfrae makes light of Elizabeth-Jane's fears, although he doesn't entirely dismiss them. Unlike Henchard, Farfrae doesn't stand by impulsive judgements. Farfrae's plan to set Henchard up in a small business again shows his generosity and gratitude towards the man who was once a good friend to him, but he drops the idea when he receives confirmation of

Henchard's hostility. Farfrae tells Lucetta that he cannot understand Henchard's feelings towards him. ❂ Has Farfrae ever deliberately hurt Henchard? Has Farfrae's desire for success in business made him insensitive to other aspects of life, such as people's feelings? Notice that he speaks to Elizabeth-Jane with *the cheeriness of a superior.* ❂ Do you think Farfrae has forgotten that he was about to marry Elizabeth-Jane?

Lucetta is nervous and unsettled by Henchard's hatred of Farfrae. She is on the point of getting Farfrae to agree that they should leave Casterbridge when news arrives that the present mayor has just died and that Farfrae will succeed him. ❂ Can you think of other examples where the timing of events adds to the sense of fate being at work? (You could look at Chapters 19 and 21.)

Henchard is particularly bitter now that Farfrae is mayor. Also, he has been given the information that Farfrae opposed the plan for the seedshop – information that does not tell the whole story and does not communicate that Farfrae is grieved to give up the scheme. The bell-ringing and band-playing to celebrate Farfrae's appointment as mayor goads Henchard further so that he decides to use Lucetta's letters to hurt Farfrae. Henchard reads aloud from Lucetta's letters, stopping short when he reaches the name of the writer, intending to reveal it with a dramatic flourish. However, he doesn't disclose the name. There is tension and humour in the scene as Farfrae listens with uninterested, polite attention to the outpourings of his wife to another man, who is sitting in front of him!

Henchard could hurt Farfrae and Lucetta in the heat of the moment, but *sitting here in cold blood he could not do it.* Even he was appalled by *such a wrecking of hearts.* ❂ How does this affect your opinion of Henchard? Does it change or confirm your ideas about his character?

Farfrae notices that the style of expression in the letters is similar to Lucetta's way of expressing herself, but he assumes that all women in love use the same kind of language. ❂ Do you think Farfrae could have guessed who the woman was – or at least have suspected Henchard's motives for reading out the letters? After all, he has been told how much Henchard dislikes him.

Ch. 35 *Another meeting at the Ring*

◆ Lucetta has overheard Henchard reading the letters.
◆ Lucetta writes to Henchard requesting a meeting.
◆ Lucetta and Henchard meet at the Ring.

Farfrae advises Henchard to burn the letters. The irony of his comment that the letters' contents would injure the woman who is now *another man's wife* adds to the drama and tension.

Lucetta cannot bring herself to tell her husband the truth about her past. She thinks he will blame her for what happened rather than sympathize with her. ❂ What do you think of her decision to write to Henchard? In her place, would you have chosen a different method of communication? Lucetta doesn't think about the risk involved in meeting Henchard secretly. She is desperate to conceal her past, yet does not think about the possible consequences of her actions.

❂ Which character does this remind you of? Look at the way Lucetta dresses for the meeting, selecting plain clothes and neglecting to heighten her natural attractions. ❂ In what ways are clothes and appearance important to Lucetta? How do she and Elizabeth-Jane differ in this respect? Lucetta asks Henchard to meet her at the Ring. ❂ What significance does this place have for Henchard?

The huge enclosure of the Ring and Lucetta's plain, entreating appearance remind Henchard of Susan, and he reproaches himself for thinking of harming a weak woman. Henchard is gentle and sympathetic to Lucetta's situation. When Lucetta begs him not to destroy her happiness Henchard feels ashamed and loses all desire to humiliate her. He promises to return the letters. Henchard almost envies Lucetta's love for Farfrae, and we are reminded of the lack of love in his own life.

STYLE AND LANGUAGE

The structural device of the two meetings at the Ring creates a dramatic effect. Henchard is reminded of his meeting with *another ill-used woman*, Susan (Chapter 11) in the same place, and the similarity of circumstances affects his response to Lucetta. Little did Lucetta know that her choice of meeting place would result in Henchard's softening towards her.

❂ What similarities do you find in both scenes?

A workout for your memory muscles

? Write trailers for these scenes: Lucetta hearing Henchard read out her letters; the meeting at the Ring; Henchard drinking again.

? Underline any words below that describe Lucetta.
cautious   reserved   calculating   shy   emotional
thoughtful   imprudent   plain   reckless   dramatic
impulsive   selfless   spontaneous   wicked
attractive   sensitive

? Mark each of these statements True or False
The marriage of Lucetta and Farfrae was witnessed by Jopp.
Henchard goes to live with Elizabeth-Jane.
Henchard keeps the hair guard Lucetta made for him.
Henchard sells the hair guard Lucetta made for him.
Henchard breaks his vow of abstinence in the King's Arms.
Farfrae offers Henchard rooms in his house.
Henchard reads extracts from Lucetta's letters out loud to Farfrae.

There's another encounter with Jopp coming up. Have a break first.

Ch. 36 *A plan and a stranger*

◆ Jopp asks Lucetta to recommend him to Farfrae; she brushes him off.
◆ Henchard asks Jopp to deliver the parcel of letters to Lucetta.
◆ Before delivering them, Jopp reads them out at Peter's Finger.
◆ A stranger arrives.

Jopp's appearances always threaten trouble. ✪ Why does he mention Jersey to Lucetta? Jopp already resents Henchard and Farfrae; now he has reason to dislike Lucetta. The background presence of the angry and frustrated Jopp with his potentially dangerous knowledge of the Jersey connection creates suspense.

Henchard has not sealed the package properly, just as Susan had not carefully sealed the letter about Elizabeth-Jane's parentage. This device is to take some blame away from those reading the letters. Notice that Jopp puts two and two together in a way that Farfrae fails to.

The company at Peter's Finger, although hardly *respectable* itself, decides to shame Lucetta by staging a skimmington-(skimmity-) ride. This is an old practice in which a bad or unfaithful husband or wife (in the Casterbridge area it is usually the wife) is mocked and ridiculed in a procession through the neighbourhood. ✪ Are you surprised that no-one defends Lucetta? Notice that the furmity woman, whose presence always means trouble for Henchard, has settled in this part of the area.

Hardy expands his depiction of life in Casterbridge with his presentation of Mixen Lane. This lane and its surroundings are inhabited by those *in distress, and in debt, and trouble of every kind*. Not only do thieves and poachers live here, but so do *pure and virtuous* people such as families who have been forced to leave their villages because they have lost the leases on their homes. The description adds to our awareness of how rural life is changing.

The stranger who arrives contributes money to the skimmington-ride and then makes his way towards town. The language used to describe his arrival and appearance gives clues as to his identity. ✪ What words and phrases suggest who the stranger is?

Ch. 37 *Royal visit* ⚔

◆ Henchard asks to be part of the welcome for a visiting royal personage.
◆ His request refused, Henchard gives his own welcome.
◆ Farfrae orders Henchard away.
◆ Solomon Longways and Christopher Coney plan a warning about the skimmity-ride.

We see the contrast between Henchard and Farfrae, the former Mayor dressed shabbily in the *weather-beaten garments of yesteryear* and the present Mayor smart and shining in his official dress. Henchard's request to join the reception seems to be a pathetic clinging-on to his old position, while Farfrae's action in dragging Henchard away from the scene emphasizes his mayoral authority. ✪ How do you react to Henchard's behaviour on this occasion?

The rustics' comments about Farfrae and Lucetta show that the pair are not popular. Although Farfrae is still liked, some of his charm has lessened as his business success has increased. Lucetta's fine clothes are criticized; notice Buzzford's comment about a *better looking woman* who is ignored. We are kept aware of Elizabeth-Jane's superiority to Lucetta.

Longways and Coney decide to warn those *most concerned* to keep out of the way when the skimmington-ride takes place. They think that the plan is rough and dangerous, and that Farfrae and Lucetta, *right enough* people, don't deserve such treatment. Notice Longways's comment that Lucetta's past is not their business. ✪ There hasn't been a skimmity-ride in Casterbridge for 10 years. Why do you think the custom is being resurrected for this particular situation?

Ch. 38 *The fight*

◆ Henchard fights Farfrae in the granary loft.
◆ Henchard overpowers Farfrae, but cannot bring himself to kill him.
◆ Henchard goes to apologize to Farfrae.
◆ Henchard remembers hearing that Farfrae was going to Weatherbury.

Henchard is angry and humiliated by Farfrae's treatment of him, and his feelings are made worse when he hears Lucetta deny that he had helped Farfrae get a footing in Casterbridge. Added to this, Lucetta has made it clear that she will not acknowledge him in public. Henchard wants revenge: *But he shall pay for it, and she shall be sorry.* Look at his list of complaints against Farfrae: *'your rivalry, which ruined me, and your snubbing, which humbled me, but your hustling, that disgraced me, I won't stand!'* ✪ Do you think Henchard's feelings are justified? Are these complaints enough to justify killing Farfrae?

Henchard ties one arm to his side, because he is the stronger man and wants to make the fight fair. Although he gains the upper hand, he does not kill Farfrae. Henchard is overcome with shame and self-reproach and wants to ask Farfrae's pardon for the attack. ✪ On what other occasion did Henchard draw back from hurting Farfrae?

Henchard's feelings for Farfrae are complex. When Farfrae approaches the granary he is humming a song he had sung at the Three Mariners when he first arrived. ✪ What are Henchard's feelings when he hears the tune? What does Henchard say when Farfrae tells him to kill him, as he's wished to long enough? Is 'hatred' an adequate description of Henchard's feelings for Farfrae?

Ch. 39 *The skimmity-ride*

◆ Lucetta watches the skimmity-ride through the window.
◆ Lucetta recognizes the effigies and falls down in a fit.
◆ The doctor orders Farfrae to be sent for.

◆ Grower rounds up helpers to stop the spectacle, but the show disappears.

Farfrae's supporters prevent him from seeing the procession by writing an anonymous letter to get him out of the way, but Lucetta receives no such protection. ❂ Why are Lucetta and Farfrae not treated in the same way? Is it just to do with character? Do you think the character's gender is an influence?

In spite of Elizabeth-Jane's attempts to protect her from the sight, Lucetta insists on watching the procession. ❂ On what other dramatic occasion was Elizabeth-Jane able to help Lucetta? Presumably Lucetta's fit is brought on by her shock and emotional reaction to the sight. ❂ What emotions does Lucetta experience as she watches? Do you think the participants in the skimmity-ride expected such an extreme response?

The chapter ends on a lighter note with the humour of the officials' ineffective attempts to find the individuals involved with the ride. The landlady of Peter's Finger even gets away with saying that the tambourine is in the oven to keep it dry!

STYLE AND LANGUAGE

The description of the skimmity-ride and its consequences provides dramatic contrasts. The details of Lucetta's clothing, the white stockings and coloured shoes, even down to the green parasol, add to the vividness of the scene and make us feel Lucetta's mounting horror. A grotesque picture is created through the description of the rude music and the lights that show the figures in *lurid distinctness*. When Lucetta collapses the roars of laughter become mere ripples, and the trampling dies out *like the rustle of a spent wind*. The assembly in Peter's Finger puts on a show of innocence, seeming *mute and inoffensive*.

Ch. 40 *Lucetta's death*

◆ Henchard hears about Lucetta's illness.
◆ Henchard intercepts Farfrae's journey to give him the news, but isn't believed.
◆ A sea-captain has called on Henchard.
◆ Farfrae eventually returns and Lucetta confesses her past.
◆ Lucetta dies.

Henchard has lost his good name and his word isn't trusted. His attempts to make Farfrae's whereabouts known and to tell Farfrae that Lucetta is ill are in vain. We feel Henchard's despair and frustration as, *full of anxiety and contrition*, he tries to make amends for his attack on Farfrae.

Henchard longs for affection, and thinks that he may come to feel for Elizabeth-Jane as if she were his own child. ❂ What further clue are we given about the stranger's identity? What is the effect of his appearance just when Henchard is hoping to be closer to Elizabeth-Jane?

Ch. 41 *Another lie*

◆ Newson arrives to enquire about Elizabeth-Jane.
◆ Henchard tells him that Elizabeth-Jane is dead.
◆ Henchard regrets his lie and fears it will be discovered.
◆ Henchard is sunk in gloom and doesn't want to live any longer.
◆ Elizabeth-Jane offers to live with Henchard.

Henchard tenderly looks after Elizabeth-Jane the next morning and imagines a future *lit by her filial presence*. Newson's reappearance is a threat to Henchard's hopes for happiness – he is the only person who knows Elizabeth-Jane's parentage. Henchard lies on the impulse of a moment and can hardly believe what he has done. The thought that Newson might return and discover the truth weighs on Henchard, but fear of losing Elizabeth-Jane, *his last treasure*, makes him persist in the deception. ❂ Do you sympathize with Henchard, or do you think he should have told the truth? Do you think that any of the lies told in the novel are justified?

Henchard is sunk so low that he intends to drown himself. He thinks he sees his own body in the river and takes this as a sign that he should not carry out his intention. What he sees is his skimmity-ride effigy that was thrown in the river and by chance has floated to that very spot. Fate and Henchard's own superstitious nature save him on this occasion.

Elizabeth-Jane's perceptive and loving nature enable her to sense Henchard's suffering and she realizes what he had intended. Her offer to live with Henchard shows her generous and forgiving spirit.

Testing times

? Mark each inn with 1st, 2nd or 3rd to show its status in Casterbridge. Write a caption for each to show the characters and types of people who frequent it.

? Explain the significance of the objects below to the story.

? Write a short obituary of Lucetta for the *Casterbridge Chronicle*.

? Make your final comments on the furmity woman's appearances.

Ch. 42 *Farfrae and Elizabeth-Jane*

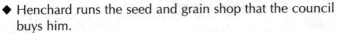

◆ Henchard runs the seed and grain shop that the council buys him.
◆ Farfrae becomes interested in Elizabeth-Jane.
◆ Henchard dislikes their relationship.

Henchard and Elizabeth-Jane enjoy *much serenity* in their new life together, although Henchard fears that she does not feel the same affection for him as she used to. Henchard shows some self-control in not opposing the relationship between Farfrae and Elizabeth-Jane. He is afraid that he will lose Elizabeth-Jane, but does not want to alienate her by speaking his mind. Elizabeth-Jane is essential to Henchard's happiness. For her sake he has humbled himself enough to accept the offer of the small business in spite of Farfrae's involvement in the arrangement.

Although Lucetta's death has brought sorrow to Farfrae, he feels that after the revelation of her past their life would not have been very happy. ✪ Are you surprised that Farfrae turns his attentions to Elizabeth-Jane? Does Farfrae have deep feelings?

Ch. 43 *Henchard leaves Casterbridge*

◆ Henchard sees Newson return.
◆ Henchard, dressed once more as a hay-trusser, leaves Casterbridge.
◆ Elizabeth-Jane meets Newson and learns that he is her real father.
◆ Plans for the wedding of Farfrae and Elizabeth-Jane go ahead.

The general opinion at the Three Mariners is that the romance between Farfrae and Elizabeth-Jane is a good thing. Christopher Coney says that it is Elizabeth-Jane who is stooping to Farfrae's level. He points out that she is independent, well-liked and sensible. ✪ What is your opinion? Which character do you admire more, Elizabeth-Jane or Farfrae? Do you think that their marriage will provide a happy ending?

Henchard watches the lovers' meetings on the Budmouth Road through a telescope from the vantage point of an ancient fort. The shock of Newson's return, seen through the telescope, is made sharper by Henchard's expectation that the figure he sees will be Farfrae. Henchard knows that the truth will come out, and *like a condemned man*, accepts his fate.

Henchard's parting words to Elizabeth-Jane are emotional. He asks her not to forget him and not to let his sins come between them. Henchard leaves behind his life at Casterbridge, the prosperity of which town he has contributed to for 20 years, in the clothes of his old trade. Watched by Elizabeth-Jane, he walks across the moor, forming much the same picture as when he arrived in Casterbridge all those years ago. ✪ Read the description of Henchard's departure. How has his appearance changed? What are your feelings for Henchard at this point?

Elizabeth-Jane does determine to forget Henchard when she hears how he lied to keep Newson away. Newson himself is good-natured and forgiving, showing some compassion for

Henchard. Newson agrees to attend the wedding only because Henchard will not be there. He is sensitive to Henchard's feelings. Farfrae is *rather uneasy* at Henchard's departure, but the general feeling is one of relief and anticipation of the forthcoming celebration. ❂ What do you think of Elizabeth-Jane's *revulsion of feeling*? Do you think Henchard should be forgiven?

Ch. 44 *Full circle*

◆ Henchard arrives back at Weydon Priors.
◆ Henchard finds work as a hay-trusser.
◆ Henchard hears that the wedding will be on St Martin's Day.
◆ Henchard goes to Casterbridge with a caged goldfinch for Elizabeth-Jane.
◆ Elizabeth-Jane rejects Henchard.

A solitary and pathetic figure, Henchard finds himself back at the very spot where he sold Susan. Henchard thinks constantly of Elizabeth-Jane, and decides to find work within range of Casterbridge. He carries with him mementos of Elizabeth-Jane, and dwells on what she might be doing. He mocks himself for feeling so strongly *about a daughter who is no daughter* of his. Henchard is in deep despair, aware of all he has lost through his own fault. It is a cruel twist of fate that Henchard gains the awareness and knowledge that would enable him to make a new and better life, but at the same time loses the will to do so.

Henchard persuades himself that Elizabeth-Jane would want him at the wedding. His isolation is emphasized as he enters the house by the back door, first leaving the goldfinch under a bush, and watches the wedding festivities through a doorway. ❂ What other scenes are seen through the frame of a window or door?

Elizabeth-Jane rejects Henchard's plea that she should *save a little room* for him in her heart. She says that she cannot love a man who has behaved in such a way. ❂ How do you react to Elizabeth-Jane's treatment of Henchard here? Henchard almost begins to explain his behaviour, but his self-esteem is so low that he cannot try to defend himself. Instead he leaves, saying that he will not bother Elizabeth-Jane to his dying day. **O** What might Henchard have said in his defence? Look at the description of his thoughts at the end of the chapter to remind you.

Ch. 45 *Henchard's death*

- ◆ Newson settles in Budmouth.
- ◆ Elizabeth-Jane realizes the significance of the dead bird in the garden.
- ◆ Elizabeth-Jane discovers that Henchard had been living with Abel Whittle.
- ◆ Henchard has died.
- ◆ Henchard's will asks that he should be forgotten.

Elizabeth-Jane's heart softens towards Henchard when she finds the dead goldfinch, and she sets out to find him to make her peace. The bird, forgotten and starved of love, is a sad reminder of Henchard himself, who dies weak and not eating, separated from his beloved Elizabeth-Jane. Our memory of the bird images in Chapter 1 heightens the effect of events having moved in a circle. He dies unaware of Elizabeth-Jane's affection for him, half an hour before Elizabeth-Jane arrives.

O What if Elizabeth-Jane had arrived in time? What difference would that make to your response to the novel as a whole?

Abel Whittle is kind to Henchard in return for the kindness that Henchard had shown his mother. Whittle is influenced by the good Henchard has done. **O** Has Henchard always been fair to Abel Whittle? Does Whittle bear a grudge? Which characters in the novel do you think are most generous in their judgement of others?

Farfrae agrees to help Elizabeth-Jane in her search for Henchard, but when they have spent a day travelling and making enquiries, he persuades her to make for home. **O** Are you surprised at Farfrae's attitude here? Is it typical of him? What is your final judgement of Farfrae? Notice that Elizabeth-Jane respects Henchard's last requests about his funeral for his sake, not so that Farfrae would have a chance to show his *large-heartedness*. **O** Does Elizabeth-Jane understand her husband's character?

Elizabeth-Jane's position at the end of the novel means that she has much to be thankful for. She has made the most of *limited opportunities* and has the security of marriage to Farfrae. However, her painful experiences have taught her that life is unfair and uncertain. The novel ends with the sombre reflection that life is a *general drama of pain* with the occasional episode of happiness.

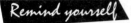

Remind yourself

?   Draw a storyboard and write the voice-overs advertising a television dramatization of the novel.

?   Imagine that you are casting a production of *The Mayor of Casterbridge*. Write a couple of lines for each main character, explaining the physical type you are looking for and giving an idea of the character's personality.

Congratulations on reaching the end of the Commentary. You've earned a break.

TOPICS FOR DISCUSSION AND BRAINSTORMING

One of the best ways to revise is with one or more friends. Even if you're with someone who hardly knows the text you're studying, you'll find that having to explain things to your friend will help you to organize your own thoughts and memorize key points. If you're with someone who has studied the text, you'll find that the things you can't remember are different from the things your friend can't remember – so you'll help each other.

Discussion will also help you to develop interesting new ideas that perhaps neither of you would have had alone. Use a brainstorming approach to tackle any of the topics listed below. Allow yourself to share whatever ideas come into your head – however silly they seem. This will get you thinking creatively.

Whether alone or with a friend, use Mind Mapping (see p. vii) to help you brainstorm and organize your ideas. If with a friend, use a large sheet of paper and thick coloured pens.

Any of the topics below could feature in an exam paper, but even if you think you've found one in your actual exam, be sure to answer the precise question given.

TOPICS

1 Do you think that Michael Henchard's downfall is caused more by fate or by his own character and actions?
2 For which of the main female characters do you feel most sympathy?
3 What does Hardy's use of place and setting contribute to the novel?
4 'In spite of his faults, Henchard manages to retain the reader's sympathy.' Do you agree?
5 Do you think that the plot of *The Mayor of Casterbridge* depends too much on chance and coincidence?
6 Take a dramatic episode from the novel and explain how its effect is created.

HOW TO GET AN 'A' IN ENGLISH LITERATURE

In all your study, in coursework, and in exams, be aware of the following:

- **Characterization** – the characters and how we know about them (e.g. what they say and do, how the author describes them), their relationships, and how they develop.
- **Plot and structure** – what happens and how it is organized into parts or episodes.
- **Setting and atmosphere** – the changing scene and how it reflects the story (e.g. a rugged landscape and storm reflecting a character's emotional difficulties).
- **Style and language** – the author's choice of words, and literary devices such as imagery, and how these reflect the mood.
- **Viewpoint** – how the story is told (e.g. through an imaginary narrator, or in the third person but through the eyes of one character – 'She was furious – how dare he!').
- **Social and historical context** – influences on the author (see 'Background' in this guide).

Develop your ability to:

- Relate **detail** to **broader content, meaning and style**.
- Show understanding of the author's **intentions, technique and meaning** (brief and appropriate comparisons with other works by the same author will gain marks).
- Give **personal response and interpretation**, backed up by **examples** and short **quotations**.
- **Evaluate** the author's achievement (how far does the author succeed and why?)

Make sure you:

- Know how to use **paragraphs** correctly.
- Use a wide range of **vocabulary** and **sentence structure**.
- Use **short** appropriate **quotations** as evidence of your understanding of that part of the text.
- Use **literary terms** to show your understanding of what the author is trying to achieve with language.

THE EXAM ESSAY

Planning

You will probably have about an hour for one essay. It is worth spending about ten minutes planning it. An excellent way to do this is in the three stages below.

1 **Mind Map** your ideas, without worrying about their order yet.
2 **Order** the relevant ideas (the ones that really relate to the question) by numbering them in the order in which you will write the essay.
3 **Gather** your evidence and short quotes.

You could remember this as the **MOG** technique.

Then write the essay, allowing five minutes at the end for checking relevance, and spelling, grammar and punctuation.

REMEMBER!

Stick to the question, and always **back up** your points with evidence in the form of examples and short quotations. Note: you can use '. . .' for unimportant words missed out in a quotation.

Model answer and plan

The next (and final) chapter consists of an answer to an exam question on *The Mayor of Casterbridge*, with the Mind Map and essay plan used to write it. Don't be put off if you don't think you could write an essay like this yet. You'll develop your skills if you work at them. Even if you're reading this the night before the exam, you can easily memorize the MOG technique in order to do your personal best.

The model answer and plan are good examples to follow, but don't learn them by heart. It's better to pay close attention to the wording of the question you choose to answer in the exam, and allow Mind Mapping to help you to think creatively.

Before reading the answer, you might like to do a plan of your own to compare with the example. The numbered points, with comments at the end, show why it's a good answer.

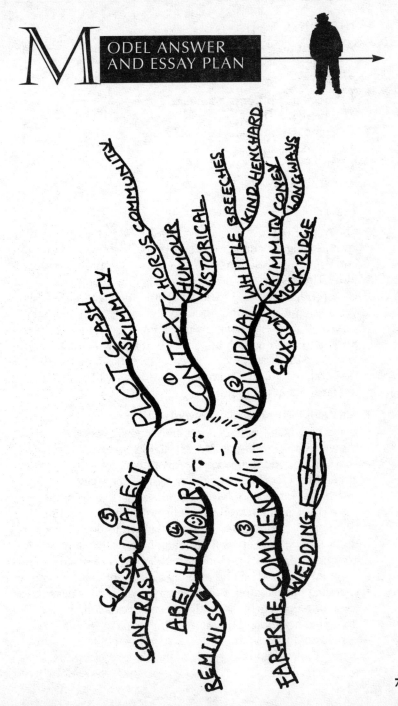

CONTEXT ① — CHORUS COMMUNITY, HUMOUR, HISTORICAL

PLOT CLASH — SKIMMITY

INDIVIDUAL ② — WHITTLE BREECHES, KIND HENSHARD, SUXSOM SKIMMITY COREY, MOCKRIDGE, LONGWAYS

CLASS DIALECT ⑤ — CONTRAST

ABEL HUMOUR ④ — REMINISC

FARFRAE COMMENT ③ — WEDDING

QUESTION
What part do the rustics play in *The Mayor of Casterbridge*?

PLAN
1 Social and historical context.
2 Different rustic characters.
3 Comment on characters and events.
4 Add humour.
5 Add realism – use of dialect.
6 Contribution to plot.

ESSAY

The role of the rustics in the novel is to act as a kind of chorus, commenting on characters and events. They also add humour and some light relief, as well as making a contribution to the plot.[1] The rustics are the ordinary working people who inhabit Casterbridge along with the affluent farmers and professionals. We are reminded of their poverty by details such as Mother Cuxsom's mother having been rewarded by the Agricultural Society for having had the largest number of healthy children without parish assistance.[2] They represent another section of the rural, agricultural community, adding realism and breadth to Hardy's depiction of life in a country town.

Although the rustics may be spoken of as a single group, the group consists of well-defined individuals.[3] Abel Whittle is shown to be a good-natured unreliable workman who can't get up in the mornings. He lives with his mother and is grateful for Henchard's kindness to her. Abel plays a crucial role in our understanding of both Henchard and Farfrae as we see each man characterized by his treatment of Abel in Chapter 15.[4] Christopher Coney is shown to be rather rambling in his thought and speech although he does make pointed comments on occasion. Solomon Longways refers to Coney's 'random way o' speaking'. Coney's matter-of-fact removal and spending of the pennies that weigh down Susan's eyes is seen to be prudent rather than callous. Longways' judgement that 'money is scarce and throat gets dry' leads us to this conclusion. Coney and Longways show thoughtfulness in getting Farfrae out of the way of the skimmington-ride, whereas Charl in Peter's Finger is ready to rob Newson of his gold. Mother Cuxsom, who asks for another song from Farfrae at the Three Mariners is jolly and warm-hearted, in contrast with the sharp-tongued Nance Mockridge, who exhibits Henchard's bad bread in public.

The rustics' comments add to our perception of what is going on. Christopher Coney's question to Farfrae about why he left his own country if he's so fond of it makes us aware of Farfrae's shallow sentimentality. When the rustics watch the royal reception in Chapter 37 Coney remarks on how much Farfrae's position has changed, and dryly points out how quickly he and Lucetta marry.[5] Their views on the marriage of Henchard and Susan make us aware of how odd the union seems to the townspeople who, of course, know nothing of the couple's history. Mother Cuxsom's tender words at Susan's death not only focus on the 'poor soul', but also heighten our awareness of the novel's sense of futility and mortality: 'her wishes and ways will all be as nothing!'[6]

However,[7] the rustics also add humour and light relief. At Henchard's wedding they reminisce about their own celebrations when they were younger. The details about drinking and falling over in the cow-barton are amusing, and also highlight the joyless nature of the present wedding. Although the episode about Abel's breeches has a serious aspect there is also the amusing description of how he would tie a string round his toe and leave the end hanging out of the window for one of his friends to tug and so wake him up.[8]

Abel, like the other rustics, speaks in the local dialect. Their way of speaking indicates their lack of education and provides a contrast with the language used by Hardy the narrator and the other characters. Abel says of his late rising 'I've fretted my gizzard green about it' and refers to the 'scantling' of cheese he had before he went to bed. The use of dialect adds realism and colour to the novel. Elizabeth-Jane sometimes uses 'pretty and picturesque' dialect words that Henchard strongly objects to, thinking that such language demeans her. This indicates how closely language was connected with class and status.[9]

The rustics also contribute to the plot. They plan the skimmity-ride that leads to Lucetta's death. Abel Whittle's late rising is the cause of the first major clash between Henchard and Farfrae. At the end of the novel Abel takes care of Henchard in his dying days, finding an empty house to give him shelter and making him as comfortable as possible. Through Abel we are reminded of Henchard's generous spirit.

The rustics, therefore, contribute to the novel's social, historical and literary content. Their life and humanity provides colour and contrast.[10]

WHAT'S SO GOOD ABOUT IT?

1 Opening focuses on question.
2 Shows awareness of historical context.
3 Point illustrated with examples.
4 Makes point about literary content.
5 Examples back up point.
6 Shows awareness of mood and tone.
7 Moves on neatly to next paragraph.
8 Knowledge of content well used.
9 Shows awareness of social context.
10 Neat relevant conclusion.

GLOSSARY OF LITERARY TERMS

alliteration   repetition of a sound at the beginnings of words, e.g. *ladies' lips.*

context   the social and historical influences on the author.

foreshadowing   an indirect warning of things to come, often through imagery.

image   a word picture used to make an idea come alive; e.g. a **metaphor**, **simile**, or **personification** (see separate entries).

imagery   the kind of word picture used to make an idea come alive.

irony   (1) where the author or a character says the opposite of what they really think, or pretends ignorance of the true facts, usually for the sake of humour or ridicule; (2) where events turn out in what seems a particularly inappropriate way, as if mocking human effort.

metaphor   a description of a thing as if it were something essentially different but also in some way similar (e.g. *And yet the seed that was to lift the foundation of this friendship was at that moment taking root in a chink of its structure* (Ch. 15)

personification   a description of something (e.g. fate) as if it were a person.

setting   the place in which the action occurs, usually affecting the atmosphere; e.g. the Three Mariners or the Ring.

simile   a comparison of two things which are different in most ways but similar in one important way; e.g. *It was compact as a box of dominoes* (Ch. 4)

structure   how the plot is organized.

theme   an idea explored by an author; e.g. time and change.

viewpoint   how the story is told; e.g. through action, or in discussion between minor characters.

NDEX